A GIFT OF HOPE

The Tony Melendez Story

A GIFT OF HOPE
The Tony Melendez Story

Tony Melendez
with Mel White

TOE JAM MUSIC
P.O. BOX 856
BRANSON, MO 65615

TO MY FAMILY,
whose love and devotion to me
has taught me to love others.

José Melendez Sr., Dad

Sara Melendez, Mom

José Melendez Jr., Brother

Mayella Romano, Sister

Mary Lou Boone, Sister

May the Lord always watch over you
and your families forever.

Contents

Acknowledgments

A special thanks to all of those mentioned in these pages. Both friends and family, you have touched my life much more than these words could ever express.

Thank you, mom and dad Zechman (my in-laws), for believing that a book about my life could inspire the lives of others. Your generosity and faith in me has gone way beyond just a simple thank you.

Thank you, Honey (my wife Lynn), for supporting, loving, and believing in me. Life without you would be empty. I truly love you with all my heart. Your love and trust is the key to our relationship with each other and especially in our daily life.

Thank you, José, for the long hours you have worked and the sacrifice of your own personal time in order to keep my musical career alive. Together we have grown as brothers and business partners and have learned a great deal in this whirlwind of a journey.

Thank you, Mel White, who took my thoughts and feelings and made them reality in the printed word.

Thank you, Bob Angelotti, for your faith in me and the vision that helped make this book possible.

Thank you, Robin Williamson and the crew at Williamson Creative Services, who graphically created the beautiful design for the front cover. Your creativity has added so much to this book.

Most of all I would like to thank God for creating me and for giving me a story to share. "Lord bless this book for those who read it and grace them with your eternal love." Amen.

FOR PERSONAL CORRESPONDENCE:

Write to: Tony Melendez
Toe Jam Music
P.O. Box 856
Branson, MO 65615

Acknowledgements

A GIFT OF HOPE

The Tony Melendez Story

Introduction: The Papal Kiss

The white papal helicopter bearing the coat of arms of John Paul II landed near the stage entrance of the Universal Amphitheatre in Hollywood, California. I couldn't see the fleet of helicopters carrying television camera crews, secret service agents, and reporters from the world's press. But all 6,000 young people sitting in the Amphitheatre with me could hear the noisy armada as it hovered over us in the cloudless sky.

The pope had come to visit America on his 1987 tour. And on this stop in Los Angeles he was about to meet with 15,000 teenagers and young adults. Besides the 6,000 of us filling every seat in the posh red-and-gold Universal Amphitheatre, another 4,000 were packed into a cathedral in St. Louis, Missouri. In Portland, Oregon, 3,000 more were crowded into the Portland Civic Auditorium. And in the Regency Hotel in Denver, Colorado, 2,000 young people were jammed together in the spacious ballroom, awaiting the pope's appearance.

History was being made, and we could feel the excitement mounting. Through the miracle of a television satellite, youth in four different locations across the western United States would be meeting simultaneously with John Paul II to discuss the issues that concerned us. Television crews in each location projected all four congregations on giant screens. We had been talking, singing, and worshiping together for almost an hour. Now, in just moments, the pope himself would enter this "Papal Spacebridge: Satellite Youth Forum" to greet us.

I was sitting on a small raised platform about twenty steps from the primary stage, where the pope would enter. I was barefoot, and my guitar rested on the floor in front of me. Somehow the

Spacebridge planning committee had heard of my name and my music. Early in the summer they had interviewed and auditioned me. Days later I received their invitation.

"Tony, we want you to sing and play for Pope John Paul II," they said, "and for a potential television viewing audience of more than one billion people."

Just three weeks before, I had been singing on a streetcorner in Laguna Beach for townsfolk and tourists who chanced by. Occasionally they would stop to listen or place a coin in my open guitar case. Now I was sitting on a little red platform that had been built for me, waiting to perform for the spiritual leader of hundreds of millions of Catholic Christians and for a live television audience so large I couldn't even imagine it.

Suddenly he was there on the stage before me. The young people in all four cities leaped to their feet and broke into an ovation that lifted the roof and sent chills up and down my spine. I had never seen a pope in person. John Paul II was wearing his traditional white robes, a white cap, and a simple gold cross. As he walked through the crowd, greeting the enthusiastic kids in English, Spanish, and other languages I couldn't understand, the people began to chant, "We love you" and "*Te amo*, Papa." He waved, nodded his head slowly, and grinned at our wild and noisy welcome.

When the last trumpet fanfare had sounded and the crowd grew quiet at last, the pope greeted us in the name of Jesus and then invited us to pray the Lord's Prayer with him. He preached briefly about hope. "The people of hope," he said, "are those who believe that God created them for a purpose and that He will provide all their needs as they seek to fulfill His purpose in their lives."

It was the same truth that my mother had passed on to me since my earliest childhood. She had believed from the moment of my birth that God had created me with something wonderful in mind, and she never let me forget it. When I grew discouraged or wondered just how I would make it, she said simply, "Trust God, Tony. He made you, and He will take care of you."

After the pope's sermon, young leaders in all four cities asked him a series of frank, probing questions. The pope answered each one honestly and openly. He didn't beat around the bush, nor did he say what was easy or popular. And whether they agreed or not, the crowds applauded each answer with growing respect for this courageous man.

"Now, Holy Father," a young man said into the microphone, "we have a special gift that we would like to present to you."

John Paul II, sitting on a chair in the middle of the stage, turned to face the speaker. And then, as he realized that I was going to be his "special gift" that day, the pope looked directly at me.

"Our gift represents courage," the young man said, introducing me, "the courage of self-motivation and family support."

The pope nodded at those words and smiled at me.

"The gift is music," the man continued, "in a performer who says when he sings, 'I hear the Lord.'"

I moved my feet up to the strings of my guitar. The lights dimmed, and a spotlight lit up my small red platform.

"Holy Father," the young man concluded, "we are proud to present to you Tony Melendez."

The audience applauded politely as they turned in my direction. Only then did they notice that I had no arms and that I was strumming the guitar with my feet. I'm used to surprised gasps and quiet whispers, and I heard them then. But I wasn't there to impress anybody. I've never felt handicapped, let alone gifted. *You* could play the guitar with your feet if you were willing to practice hard enough. I didn't play that day because I had no arms and the program needed a novelty; I played to celebrate the presence and the power of God in each of us. And I think that the people could tell, as I sang, that I wasn't a performer at a circus. This was a singer of the Song of Songs.

I didn't look at John Paul II. I didn't think about that huge arena filled with people or about the millions watching me on television. I just closed my eyes and sang the song as a prayer to God, as always.

> "The day is filled with love.
> Today is like no other day before,
> And you and I will never be the same.

> I give you all my love this day and every day,
> Forever and forever, in our joys and in our pains."

An orchestra joined me on the second verse, and people began to clap in rhythm to the music.

> "In union with our God we are become as one.
> In him we will bring light into the dark.
> We fill the day with love.
> This day is like no other day before.
> And even more, you and I will never be the same."

It was a simple song, and I sang it from my heart. It was a gift to our visitor, to the millions watching, to my family, and especially to my Heavenly Father, whose presence makes every day like no other day before.

When I finished the song, the audience gave me a standing ovation; even the pope was standing and clapping his hands above his head enthusiastically with the crowd. It was truly a day like no other! I could have died that instant and felt my life fulfilled.

Then something totally unpredictable happened: the pope walked down from the stage. He had to descend several steps and then jump down off the edge of the platform to reach me. Security people scrambled to keep up with John Paul II's unscheduled journey, and television crews tried to follow. Hands reached out to help him.

Suddenly the pope was standing at my feet. At that moment I wished I had arms. I wanted to reach out and take his hands in mine. I wanted to lean forward and embrace him. Instead, he held his arms out to me. My heart was hammering, and my eyes were blinking back tears. As I leaned forward, the pope took my head in his hands, stood up on tiptoes, and kissed me gently on the right cheek.

The crowd of young people went wild, cheering, singing, and clapping their hands high in the air. The pope looked me in the eyes, then turned and walked back to his central place on that impressive platform.

I thought that my heart would burst. As I tried to take in what had just happened to me, we were once again surprised by this insightful man. I couldn't believe it, but John Paul II was calling my name above the cheering crowd.

"Tony," he said. But the young people wouldn't be silent.

"Tony," he repeated a second and then a third time.

Finally the people in the gigantic room grew still.

"Tony," he began a fourth time, "you are truly a courageous young man. You are giving hope to all of us. My wish to you is to continue giving this hope to all the people."

I tried not to cry, but tears brimmed up in my eyes and a few uncontrollable strays trickled down my cheek and into my beard. For the last months I had been praying for God's direction. Now Pope John Paul II himself was delivering God's word to me.

"Give hope to all the people," he had said, and a voice inside me answered, *Yes, it was for this that I was born. It was for this that I came into the world.*

1. In the Beginning

One spring night early in May 1961, my parents made love on an old featherbed in a house on stilts overlooking Lake Nicaragua. I was born nine months later with no arms, eleven toes, and a severe clubfoot. Looking back, no one can blame my parents for what happened to me during those thirty-six weeks of growth inside my mother's womb. In all probability I was conceived that night with no serious imperfections. There is no reason to doubt that my parents' genes had all the right stuff. And the tiny embryo they created out of their love for each other set about immediately to form a perfectly whole child with two normal arms and two well-shaped legs and feet. With hearts full of hope, they came together and gave me life.

Five times in the past twenty-seven years I have visited that old summer-house where life began for me. My grandparents built their little vacation hideaway just thirty minutes from their home in Rivas, Nicaragua, above the shore of the largest lake in Central America. Spanish explorers called the lake *Mar Dulce,* "sweet sea." This freshwater lake, created from a prehistoric volcanic eruption, is 110 miles long and an average of 36 miles wide and 200 feet deep. Somehow the ocean-going animals trapped in the newly formed inland sea managed to survive and adapt. (I wonder if something of their spirit was born in me.) Consequently, Lake Nicaragua is the only freshwater lake in the world containing shark, swordfish, and tarpon.

Grandpa and Grandma Rodriquez's lakefront summer-house stands a full story above the flood tide on thirty-five wooden posts anchored in cement. The weathered walls of gray pine plank are topped by a slightly sloping tin roof that deflects the sun and amplifies the drumming of tropical rains. Five screened windows look out on the lake, and a front porch long enough for boisterous games during a seasonal downpour runs the full length of the house. A giant sapodilla tree with a trunk as wide as an automobile and gnarled branches twisting five stories overhead shields the porch from summer heat and winter squalls.

When the temperature begins to rise, Grandpa and Grandma still lock up their home in nearby Rivas, pack the trunk with the weekend's supplies, and drive to their "cabin" by the lake. After their marriage my parents often borrowed the lake-house for vacations of their own.

MOM AND DAD

My mother, Sara María Rodriquez, an elementary school teacher in Rivas, often sat on the porch high above the lake, tending her first son, José Jr., born two years before my birthday and reading her Bible, textbooks, short stories, or Spanish poetry; while my father, José Angel Melendez, a college graduate in agriculture and animal husbandry, swam or fished in the lake or investigated the flora and fauna of the nearby jungles, rivers, and swamps.

Although my father was a city boy, born and raised in San Salvador, the capital of El Salvador, he loved the jungle and everything that grew in it. His father, Pablo Ramón Melendez, was a dentist whose large and successful practice was housed in the Melendez family home on a busy streetcorner in the capital. My father knew the privileges of the professional classes during his childhood and adolescence, but from his earliest days he was determined to escape into the countryside from smoggy, gray cities paved in asphalt and cement.

After attending elementary and junior high school in San Salvador, my father was accepted with honors at Nicaragua's International Academy of Agriculture in Rivas. He met my mother while both were students, courted her with flowers and serenades, and eventually won her hand in marriage. Together they explored the green, growing world of southwestern Nicaragua.

Upon graduation my father was hired by a large sugar-cane refinery in Rivas to supervise the cultivation of the cane fields growing at the edges of the jungle. He and his crews cleared the fields and planted, irrigated, and harvested the cane. In his spare time

Dad passed on to the local farmers the secrets of the soil that he had learned in agricultural school. But in every free moment he sneaked away to explore the thickly overgrown jungles around Rivas, and the little creeks, estuaries, streams, and rivers that gave those jungles life.

Dad trapped boa constrictors and (to the horror of my mother) loved to let them slither across his bare back and around his waist. He tracked spotted deer and an occasional anteater. He caught sharks in the lake and crocodiles in the marshlands. After one productive trip into the jungle, my father returned to Rivas carrying a baby crocodile in a wet gunnysack strapped on his back. As a prank he placed the crocodile at the bottom of an abandoned well in the middle of town. It was soon discovered and named Melendez, in honor of my father.

The crocodile, like its reputation in our town, grew bigger and bigger, until one stormy winter day the well overflowed and Melendez lumbered off down the main street looking for his dinner. To this day when family members return home for a visit, townspeople remind us of the crocodile named Melendez: the mascot of Rivas, who lived to a happy old age in the bottom of an abandoned well.

THE LAND OF MARVELS

Nicaraguans call our nation *Tierra de Maravillas,* "the land of marvels." Every day was a new adventure for my father, who had determined to discover each new *maravilla* for himself. You must visit Nicaragua to understand his fascination with the emerald-green and sapphire-blue splendor of Nicaragua's nearly 50,000 square miles. And though he never tired of exploring the wonder of Mexico and of all the neighboring nations of Central America, Nicaragua especially captured my father's heart.

On a map you will find the country of my birth in the heart of Central America: between Honduras to the northeast, El Salvador to the northwest, and Costa Rica to the south. We have 575 miles of Caribbean coastline and 215 miles of beaches and cliffs along the

Pacific Ocean. To the north, a heavily forested mountain range rises 6,000 feet along the border we share with Honduras, and a spectacular range of dormant and active volcanoes runs down the length of our Pacific coastline. Central Nicaragua is a fantasyland of rolling green hills, verdant valleys and jungles, long, wide rivers, and cascading streams all descending gently toward the Mosquito Coast, our eastern marshlands along the Caribbean.

Rivas, the town where I was born, lies in southwestern Nicaragua on a fairly narrow strip of land between Lake Nicaragua and the Pacific Ocean. Dad and Mom could drive east from Rivas to the colorful village of San Jorge to visit Grandpa's lakefront cottage or drive an hour west to the picturesque seaside resort town of San Juan del Sur, its white sandy beaches fronting on the Pacific Ocean.

Their new life together in Rivas seemed perfect for my young parents. Their future was secure. Dad loved his work. As a valued employee of a prospering refinery, he was paid well and his benefits were considerable. Dad, Mom, and José even lived free in a comfortable cottage provided them by the management of the sugarcane refinery. With his father-in-law the accountant for Rivas's only hospital, my father and his family were guaranteed excellent health and medical care. And Dad was surrounded by the *maravillas* of his newly adopted land. What more could he dream of?

Dad loved life in Nicaragua. On Saturday nights he and Mom would join their friends for dinner and animated conversation. They would walk together to their favorite local nightspot to listen to the music and to dance. My father played the guitar and sang beautifully. He organized his own guitar trio to serenade my mother and other pretty girls in the village.

While Saturday nights were times of singing and celebration for my father, almost every Sunday morning he and my mother went to the cathedral in Rivas or to church in San Jorge or San Juan del Sur to confess their sins and to pray prayers of gratitude for God's many blessings in their life. According to those who knew him best, Dad was especially grateful for his beautiful young wife and for their healthy infant son.

THE POISON CAPSULE

Neither my father nor my mother had any idea during those first weeks of summer in 1961 that they had conceived me or that I was already taking shape in the quiet safety of my mother's womb. When the early signs of pregnancy were confused with the symptoms of flu, my mother called Tío Toño, her uncle and one of Rivas's leading physicians, and described her occasional bouts with nausea and dizziness. Dr. Toño prescribed a new drug recently imported into Nicaragua from West Germany.

My mother went to the drugstore herself, bought the thalidomide capsules, and carried them home. How could she know that something prescribed by a trusted family physician and purchased from the city's finest pharmacy would deform her unborn son and alter her life and the life of our family forever?

That was in 1961, less than thirty years ago. People still believed that a newly conceived fetus was almost totally protected within its tough translucent envelope. It was assumed that the placenta could detect and screen out any dangerous substances that might be traveling in the mother's blood. Few people then even suspected that an unborn child growing in a mother's womb could be damaged by such recreational drugs as marijuana and cocaine or that smoking tobacco or drinking alcohol could cause mental retardation and physical deformity in an unborn child. And certainly nobody suspected that approved over-the-counter drugs might lead to deformity or death for the unborn. But the very year that I was born, the world would discover that truth through the tragedy of thalidomide.

Thalidomide. An ugly word. It scares people even now, twenty-seven years after it was tracked down, exposed, and put away for good in 1962. But just four years earlier, when this "miracle drug" was first introduced in West Germany in 1958, people sang its praises.

The advertising campaign selling thalidomide to people around the world claimed that West German scientists had finally discovered a chemical that helped people go to sleep quickly and calmly. They promised that the user would awaken in the morning without feeling drugged or hung over. And they guaranteed that, unlike barbiturates, it posed no danger from accidental overdose. In fact, thalidomide was considered so safe that you could gulp down bottles of the stuff without killing or even damaging yourself. Best of all, it was cheap and convenient. You could buy thalidomide over the drugstore counter without visiting the doctor for a prescription. Millions of grateful people rushed to buy and use thalidomide in Europe, Asia, and Central and South America.

In 1959, just months after thalidomide was released to an unsuspecting world, terribly deformed babies were born in cities across West Germany. According to a fascinating article by William Grigg in the *FDA Consumer* magazine (February 1987), pictures and X-rays of these "grossly deformed" infants were shown at a medical meeting in 1960. Their mysterious condition, rare in all the world until that time, was called *phocomelia*, a combination of the Greek words for "lamb" and "seal." Dr. Grigg writes that "malformed fingers or toes appeared at the ends of very foreshortened limbs—making them look like flippers." Thus the label "lambs that look like seals."

The exhibit shocked and stimulated the doctors, of course, but no one made the connection between this sudden rash of misshapen infants and thalidomide, the new miracle drug that those same doctors were prescribing to their pregnant patients. Meanwhile, the William S. Merrell Company had submitted an application to produce and market thalidomide in the United States, and according to Dr. Grigg, studies "proving" the safety of thalidomide filled four books the size of a Chicago telephone directory.

THE MIRACLE OF DR. FRANCES KELSEY

Thank God that request to market thalidomide in the United States was never approved. The application was laid on the desk of a new employee of the Food and Drug Administration. Dr. Frances Kelsey, a physician and pharmacologist, was given the usual sixty days to review the thalidomide application and to decide upon its merits.

"It was deemed to be a simple application," she recalled to William Grigg, "and since I had just reported to work, it was assigned to me."

The applicant pharmaceutical company thought that thalidomide would be approved without event. But Dr. Kelsey proved them wrong. She was especially troubled by the fact that the drug worked differently in animals than in people. "Why would it induce sleep in human beings and not in animals?" she remembers wondering. "It was a very unusual kind of drug and we had no idea how it worked."

Her uneasy feelings about thalidomide led Dr. Kelsey to ask a series of questions of scientists supporting the drug's application and of neutral scientists, both inside and outside the Food and Drug Administration. No amount of pressure could dissuade Dr. Kelsey from her search to discover the truth about thalidomide.

In the meantime eighty-three deformed infants had been born in West Germany. Still there were no apparent reasons to suspect thalidomide as the cause of those deformities. Fortunately, release of the drug was still being stalled in America by Dr. Kelsey and the FDA.

Coincidentally, Dr. Kelsey and her husband, F. Ellis Kelsey, had teamed up to do their own research on the effects of chemicals on the unborn child. It showed that "embryos developed the capacity to produce various enzymes for breaking down certain chemicals at various stages in their growth. Thus, if a certain enzyme hadn't been produced yet, the unborn child could not process certain chemicals that an adult or a more mature fetus could."

In February 1961 Dr. Kelsey noticed an article in a British medical journal that reported "tingling nerve inflammations in the fingers of patients who had taken thalidomide for a long time."

After reading the article and thinking about its implications, the newly employed FDA scientist wondered to herself if "this painful tingling and numbness of the extremities in an adult might have a parallel in the fetus." One question led to another, until Dr. Kelsey finally asked herself and her colleagues, "Could harm come to the unborn infant if the mother took the drug during pregnancy?"

While Dr. Kelsey was struggling with her research in America, the outbreak of phocomelia in Europe had become an epidemic. Hundreds of deformed babies were being born. William Grigg summarizes their condition: "Some infants had no legs at all, just toes sprouting from their hips, along with fore-shortened, flipper like arms. Some people blamed radioactive fallout from atom bomb testing," Dr. Grigg recalls. "Others thought abnormal chromosomes might be to blame, or X-rays of the mother while she was pregnant."

Still no one blamed thalidomide, until a West German doctor in Hamburg, Dr. Widukind Lenz, established the connection with a survey in his own clinic. Twenty percent of the mothers bringing deformed infants to his clinic remembered having taken thalidomide during their pregnancy. A doctor in Australia reported similar connections between infant deformities and the drug. After retesting the mothers with specific questions about thalidomide, the number of those remembering that they had taken the drug during pregnancy increased to more than fifty percent.

In November 1961 thalidomide was recalled in Germany. That same year, the application to market thalidomide in America was withdrawn. Just a few months after my mother purchased that small bottle of thalidomide capsules from her pharmacist in Rivas, a massive recall of the drug was mounted across the world. But the truth about thalidomide was discovered too late for thousands of infants born misshapen and deformed.

In just four years—between 1959 and 1963—more than 10,000 deformed infants were born without arms or legs in nations around the world. The real extent of the suffering caused by thalidomide to these children and their families was just beginning to be discovered.

Few people realized how close this country had come to a terrible disaster until Dr. Helen B. Taussig, professor of pediatrics at

Johns Hopkins University, made the connection. The William Grigg article notes that after a study tour of Europe she announced to the American press, "This compound [thalidomide] could have passed our present drug laws." On July 15, 1962, a reporter added, "This is the story of how the skepticism and stubbornness of a government physician prevented what could have been an appalling American tragedy, the birth of hundreds or indeed thousands of armless and legless children."

In 1962, the year I was born, a landmark drug law was passed by Congress that would help prevent such tragedy from ever happening in America. At the signing of the bill, President John F. Kennedy awarded Dr. Frances Kelsey the Distinguished Federal Civilian Service Award. "Through high ability and steadfast confidence in her professional decision," the award reads, "she has made an outstanding contribution to the protection of the health of American people."

"WHAT HAPPENED TO MY BABY?"

My mother remembers taking several thalidomide pills, throughout a two-week period. At the end of the two weeks, in the summer of 1961, my parents left for their summer vacation to El Salvador, and Mom forgot the bottle of thalidomide capsules in Rivas, but the chemical had entered her bloodstream and I hadn't developed sufficiently inside her to fight off the poison. The damage had been done, and there was no way to undo it.

At four in the morning on January 9, 1962, I was born in the little hospital in Rivas. My mother's uncle, Dr. Toño, returned to his private office after delivering me and wept. About eight that same morning, my mother awakened with my Grandma at her side in the recovery room. None of the family were bustling about, grinning, and patting her hand as they had when José was born. A nurse came in to attend her.

"I want to see my baby," my mother demanded.

"You *will* see him," the nurse answered gently. Then, as she hurried from the room, she added an unconvincing, "Don't worry. Everything will be all right."

But my mother remembers worrying a lot that morning. She knew immediately that something had gone wrong. In Nicaragua, after delivery a mother cradles her newborn child. She is immediately responsible for nursing and changing the infant. To lie alone in the maternity ward after giving birth is a sure sign of tragedy. And no one had the courage to tell my mother exactly what had happened.

"Did he die?" my mother asked the next person who entered her room.

"No, he didn't die," the orderly answered. "He's alive. Don't worry."

My poor mother: no one would tell her the truth. And my poor family? They had gathered with joy and excitement for my birth. My father, grandparents, uncles, aunts, and cousins had come to the hospital armed with flowers and gifts, ready to celebrate my entry into the world. But when they saw me, born with no arms and a clubfoot bent back grotesquely against my leg, the flowers and gifts were put away and the excited chatter was replaced by an embarrassed silence. Finally my grandmother called the whole family into an emergency huddle.

"Sara is exhausted from the birth," someone suggested. "She shouldn't see this baby in her condition."

"This baby won't live," someone else added. "We must call a priest."

"How did it happen?" everyone was asking. "How could two such healthy people give birth to an armless, crippled child?"

Finally the family agreed what must be done: a priest was called. I would be baptized and last rites would be given. It looked as if my first birthday would be my last. The family was preparing me to die.

One by one, people drifted into my mother's room.

"Where's my baby?" she asked each of them. "What have you done with him?"

Finally, after hurried telephone calls to make all the last-minute arrangements, my father sat down on the edge of my mother's hospital bed. Gently he cradled her in his arms.

"What's wrong with my baby?" she whispered hoarsely.

"The baby is fine, Saruca," he lied quietly, hoping to calm her. "He's okay. He just has a problem . . ."

For a moment he paused, trying to find the appropriate words. Finally he found strength to continue. "He has a problem with his leg."

"With his leg?" she prompted. "What's wrong with his leg? They can fix legs, can't they? Bring him in to me. I want to see him."

Still nobody moved toward the nursery. My mother looked around the room nervously. She remembers to this day how their silent looks of pity and condolence only made her feel worse.

"They can fix a leg," she repeated. "This isn't a problem. There must be something more. What has happened?"

My father and mother loved each other. They hadn't built their relationship on lies. He could pretend no longer. "I want to tell you the truth," he began haltingly.

Then he paused. Mom remembers that his eyes glistened with tears as he smiled down upon her sadly.

"Our baby has no arms," he said. For a moment he paused as if he were going to say more. Then quickly he turned away and began to sob.

Imagine how much more he wanted to say to her. I know my father's heart. He was young and strong. Until that moment life had had no limits. He was trained in agriculture and animal husbandry. His hands were skilled and efficient. Around the house, at his work in the refinery or in the cane fields near Rivas, he could fix almost anything. Something might be done to straighten the twisted clubfoot. But there were no arms—not even stumps in my shoulders where arms should have been. And that he couldn't fix.

Then, up against their sense of loss and failure, he wanted to comfort her, to give her words of hope, to promise that something good might come from all this. But at that moment he felt no hope. What possible good could come from such a tragic birth? That's when he turned away.

For a moment my mother looked around the room in shock and sadness. Then she too began to cry. About that time Grandma Rodriquez returned to my mother's room.

"What's going on here?" she asked. My mom and dad were crying. My grandfather, my uncles and aunts, even my cousins were in tears. Immediately Grandma walked up to my mother's side, took out her own lace handkerchief, and began to wipe her daughter's tears away.

"This is no time for crying," she said firmly. "God has sent us this baby. And God knows what he's doing."

My mother remembers that her sadness disappeared even as Grandma spoke. Mom knew nothing about thalidomide. She had no idea what had deformed me or what might be done about it. She didn't even know if I would live or die. But this one thing she knew for certain: God was alive and present in her life. She would trust him for her future, for the future of her family, and for the future of the little armless baby she had just delivered.

Mom remembers taking my father's hand and squeezing it. He turned back toward her and wiped away his tears. Her dark-brown eyes sparkled once again. Her shocked and frightened look had disappeared, and her tears were wiped away.

"I felt strong," she told me recently. "I knew that God had sent you to us for a reason. And I leaned back against the pillow feeling God's presence in the room. The journey ahead was uncertain, but arms or no arms, I knew that God would be with you and us every step along the way."

At that moment Dad leaned down, kissed my mother on the forehead, and embraced her. He couldn't know the long hard days and terrible nights that lay ahead for both of them; but her hope was contagious, and he felt it growing in his own heart even as he held her in his arms.

2. The Red Balloon

My mother didn't see me until I was five days old. Her doctor and her parents were afraid that the shock of seeing me might do her harm. But Mother proved them wrong. She remembers that first day when I was brought from the hospital nursery in a light-blue blanket and placed in her open, waiting arms.

"You were wrapped up tightly in that blanket," she told me, "and they didn't want me to unwrap you. They wanted me to look at your face only. I didn't know why they were so afraid for me to see your body, since they had already told me the bad news. But you had a beautiful face," she assured me. (And how could I argue with my mother?) "Your eyes sparkled even then," she added. "So I cradled you in my arms and thanked God that you were born. But before long, holding you and looking into your eyes wasn't enough."

Actually, there's no reason to be angry at the doctor or my mother's family for keeping me from her those first few days. During that same time she was suffering from terrible leg cramps; the muscles in her calves would tighten without warning, and she would writhe in pain on the hospital bed until someone rubbed the cramps away. At the time they didn't know how much of that cramping was caused by the emotional stress my birth had caused her. Now, looking back, we know that they made a mistake in not placing me in her arms the moment I was born.

"The first time I unwrapped you," my mother told me, "I didn't know what I would feel. The doctor had warned me that I would find nothing where your arms, hands, and fingers should have been except for one tiny little finger growing out of your left shoulder. He told me that you had a small sixth toe growing out of your left foot, that your lower left leg was deformed, and that your left foot, a clubfoot, was twisted back up against your leg. It sounded terrible, but I couldn't know how I would feel about it until finally they let me see you for myself."

Twenty-seven years have passed since she unwrapped me that first time, but Mom still remembers how she felt that day as her eyes and hands set out to discover how much of me was in perfect working order and at the same time to measure the missing and damaged parts. Apparently I lay naked on the blanket, staring up at her. For several minutes her eyes scanned me from the top of my head to the tips of my eleven little toes. Then she picked me up in her arms, placed me to her breast, and began to whisper words that, though I couldn't yet understand them, would make all the difference in the months and years to come.

"José Antonio Melendez Rodriquez," she whispered, "you are a beautiful baby. God has given you so much. You have a wonderful face with dark-brown eyes, a cute little nose, pouty lips, and two tiny, perfect ears. With your eyes you will see God's gifts all around you: the bright-red parrots sitting in the coconut trees and the white clouds high up in the sky. With that little nose you will smell the flowers, and the incense and the fragrant candles burning at God's altar. With your lips you will sing songs and pray prayers to your Father in heaven. And with those perfect little ears you will hear his voice in the wind, in the sea, and in your heart telling you, 'I love you, Tony. I love you very much.'

"You are almost perfect, Antonio," she remembers whispering to me that day. "You have shiny black hair on that handsome head, a strong, proud neck, broad shoulders, a wonderful chest with a pair of healthy lungs and a beating heart, and at least one good leg to stand on. You have all the working parts you need to become a strong, beautiful man. God has great dreams for you," she said, "and he and I together will see that all those dreams come true."

Grandmother Rodriquez entered the room as Mom was cradling me in her arms and whispered into her ear. "Don't worry, Sara," she said, mistaking my mother's grateful tears for tears of panic. "We'll take Antonio up to the United States just as soon as he can travel. They'll fix him. You'll see."

My mother only smiled at her. She knew that I would need some "fixing," to be sure. Something would have to be done about my twisted leg and my clubfoot. But she also believed with all her heart that God and she were already at work "fixing" me where it counted. Somehow my mother knew that handicaps and deformities could lead to blessings or to bitterness, to life or to death. And from the beginning she decided to thank God for my weaknesses and to trust him to transform them through his love and hers into strengths.

THE GOSSIP SPREADS

"Did you hear?" one neighbor child said to another. "Mrs. Melendez had a little monster."

"Really?" another child exclaimed. "What does he look like?"

"I don't know," answered a third. "Let's go see!"

Rivas was then a compact little city of about 9,000 people. The paved highway ended at the edge of town, and you could walk the cobblestone street that passed from north to south across the entire village in less than twenty minutes. (And you didn't have to walk very fast, either.) Rumors spread even faster. In fact, it seemed that the moment I was born everyone in Rivas knew that something was wrong with me.

When word got out about the Melendez "monster," everyone was curious to see me. I suppose that's one reason my mother stayed with Grandpa and Grandma Rodriquez the first few months after I was born. Their large and comfortable home in the heart of town afforded protection from prying eyes and gossiping tongues. No one in Rivas was hateful or malicious, but children and their parents walked up and down the cobblestone street where my grandparents lived, hoping to catch a glimpse of me. After hearing Mom's stories about how hard people worked to see me, it's easier to understand why P. T. Barnum was such a success with his traveling circus of midgets, two-headed calves, and fat ladies who grew beards.

The Rodriquez house fills an entire corner of a downtown block in the heart of Rivas. A multicolored tile roof with a protective border made of corrugated iron rests upon high whitewashed walls with five sets of large double doors opening onto the sidewalk and one large picture window facing out on the cobblestone street. The outside of Grandpa's home is plain, even stark, hiding the brilliant colors and the comfortable accommodations inside those high, colorless walls.

Inside, the home is warm and comfortable with red tiled floors and long tiled hallways. The living room is large and high-ceilinged, furnished simply to my grandmother's taste with white wooden furniture, white drapes, and colorful carpets, along with oil paintings, native pottery, family pictures, trinkets, and treasures. Grandpa's combination den and office is just off the living room. Bedrooms can be found up and down the hallways.

In one bedroom hangs a huge white hammock that has rocked sleepy children and grandchildren for more than fifty years. A maid's room joins the kitchen and the dining room near the back of the house. In the courtyard green plants grow in profusion. Parakeets and parrots land in the branches of the trees, and beautiful potted flowers (including white and purple orchids) seem always to be blooming.

From the outside the house looks more like a fortress than a home. Those high white walls keep out summer heat and winter cold—and prying eyes in every season. The family thought that my mother and I would be safer there than in the little company cottage my father and mother lived in near the busy refinery on the outskirts of town. They wanted to protect me and my mother behind those high walls and locked double doors.

Mother had another idea. "Let's put our chairs in the open doorway," she said to Grandma shortly after they brought us home from the hospital.

"Whatever for?" Grandma asked. "The draft would be bad for little Tony."

My mother carried me toward the door and hesitated. It was common for families to push open the huge double doors and to crank open the long louvered windows early in the evening when the breezes from the lake circulated through town, cooling the cobblestones and blowing gently through the open houses. The large open doorway on the sidewalk would become a kind of porch. The family would sit together in chairs that were half in the house and half outside. They would drink fresh guava or pineapple punch and greet neighbors and friends who might be strolling by.

"You're not going to take him out there, are you?" one of my uncles asked Mother as she stood waiting.

"Your uncles were young," she explained to me later. "They had already been in fights defending you and me from the questions and the teasing of their playmates."

"You got a little monster baby in your house, Francisco?" someone would ask.

"Isn't Halloween kind of early this year?" another child would chime in.

In minutes loud threats would be exchanged and fists would be flying.

"I think the neighbors should see him," my mother said simply as she stood there waiting until the doors were opened.

"Let me hold him, then," Grandma Rodriquez said. And Mom remembers the determined look in her own mother's eyes as she sat down in the open doorway with me in her arms, daring the neighborhood children and the local town gossips to lift one eyebrow in criticism of her grandson.

At first no one ventured near, although children looked out from open windows and around doors that were cracked ajar. Then a little boy and his mother walked by. The mother smiled and tried to pass, but the child ran directly to Grandma Rodriquez, who tightened her grip on me and prepared for battle.

"Can I see him?" the child asked. "Can I see the new baby?"

Grandma hesitated. No one was about to insult her grandson—not even a six-year-old neighbor child.

Mom, however, smiled. "Of *course* you may see him," she said, taking me from Grandma's arms and sitting me up on her lap facing the curious child.

At that moment the light cotton blanket slipped away from my shoulders. Dressed only in my diaper, I lay propped in my mother's arms before the child.

"He's cute," the little boy said. "Look—he's smiling at me!"

The boy didn't seem to notice that I had no arms, eleven toes, or a twisted clubfoot.

"He's cute," the rumor spread. "Yes, he's missing a few things here and there, but he seems to be a happy baby." The new word was out. "A monster? Don't be silly. That Melendez baby is going to do fine."

From that day on, no one has ever tried to hide me or my handicaps again.

JESUS AND THE CHILDREN

On January 23, 1962, just fourteen days after I was born, my mother decided to take me to La Iglesia de San Francisco, the cathedral in Rivas, for the blessing of the children, sometimes called the Feast of the Infant Jesus of Prague.

Two thousand years ago a group of curious children interrupted our Lord in the middle of a lesson to His disciples. The grownups tried to shush the children and send them away, but Jesus stopped them: "Let the children come unto me," He told them, "and forbid them not. For of such is the kingdom of heaven."

Children were important to Jesus. He made that perfectly clear by his life and by his teachings. And because children were so important to our Lord, for the past 2,000 years children have been important to His church. In Rivas, at the beginning of every new year, a service is held to honor the children and to dedicate them to our Lord's service. Special dresses are made for the girls, and the boys' white shirts and dark pants are cleaned and pressed. Shoes are shined. Hair is washed and combed into place. And the cathedral is filled with noisy children and their parents for the dedication service.

Our church in Rivas, named in honor of Saint Francis, is really very special. The whitewashed walls may be streaked and an occasional earthquake crack might be seen in the leaded stained-glass windows, but those walls hold up three towers and two round, domed cupolas that are the most perfect of all the churches in

Nicaragua; and the sun shines through those colored windows to light up a sanctuary that is as beautiful and elegant as any in the world.

Mom remembers the day she ventured out into the streets of Rivas carrying me in her arms for my public debut. Small streams of children and their parents flowed down the hard dirt paths and cobblestone streets converging on Carazo Park en route to the Cathedral. A trio of guitarists played in the red-and-green gazebo in the center of town. Bright streamers of colored paper had been hung from the light poles and the trees. An ice-cream vendor rang his bell, and local merchants stood in the doorways of their little stores, calling out greetings to customers and their children.

The noisy crowd of children and their parents slowed just outside the great door of the cathedral. Only so many people could pass through the arch at one time. Mom remembers holding me tightly in the crowd as Grandma leaned over me protectively. I was a real curiosity that day. Everybody in Rivas knew that I had been born with no arms, so parents and children alike looked curiously at Mom and at the bundle she carried. People whispered and pointed in our direction. No one knew exactly how to feel about a tiny deformed baby being dedicated to God just days after his "tragic" birth.

THE INFANT JESUS OF PRAGUE

Just inside the nave of the cathedral the stream of children and their parents passed by a statue known as the Infant Jesus of Prague. Devout adults and children clinging tightly to their parents' hands bowed respectfully in the direction of the Holy Child.

You've probably seen a picture of this eighteen-inch wooden statue of the baby Jesus wearing a gold crown, a bright-red cape, and a starched white robe. He's just an infant, yet He's standing erect. He's less than a year old, yet He looks the viewer directly in the eyes with a wise, understanding gaze. No one knows who created this bright-eyed and compassionate portrayal of the infant

Jesus, but it's had a special place in Catholic tradition since the seventeenth century, when a Czechoslovakian princess gave it to the Carmelite sisters in Prague.

For a moment my mother stood gazing up at the Infant Jesus of Prague. Grandma continued into the sanctuary, thinking Mom would follow. But my mother didn't move. People crowding in around her glanced in our direction. The stream of mothers and children threatened to sweep her past that little Holy Child, yet Mom continued staring up into His eyes, holding me tightly in her arms. Finally, when the business between them was completed, my mother walked by into the candlelit cathedral.

I've asked myself often why that small statue of the infant Jesus wearing the clothing of a king meant so much to my mother in those early days of my life. (She still carries a picture of the statue in her purse these twenty-seven years later.) Now at last I think I know.

Most statues, paintings, carvings, etchings, woodcuts, and tapestries of the infant Jesus portray Him as He really was: a tiny, helpless baby wrapped in pieces of old cloth, lying on His back in a stable, waving His pudgy little arms and feet in the air. But this seventeenth-century Czech woodcarver and painter created the infant as He one day would be, with the regal bearing and the royal crown of the King of Kings. The others saw Jesus as He was; the seventeenth-century woodcarver saw Him as He one day would be.

I think that's what gave my mother hope. The other mothers and children crowding around us in the nave of the cathedral saw me as I was: a tiny, crippled, armless child. My mother saw me as I one day would be: a grown man with God's dream in his heart.

Suddenly the organist began to play, and a children's choir sang a call to worship. Mom and Grandma took their seats and joined in singing the opening hymn. I don't remember a thing about that day, but from my earliest childhood I've been thrilled by the sound of a pipe organ and children's voices echoing in a great cathedral. Maybe my love for the music of the liturgy began that day when I was just two weeks old.

THE BLESSING

Mom tells me that the priest delivered a short sermon about Jesus and His love for little children at that service long ago. Then, after another song and prayers, the mothers and fathers present were invited to bring their children to the altar individually to receive God's blessing. For the next twenty or thirty minutes, the children and their parents moved quietly down the aisles and into place across the front of the church.

"What's the baby's name?" the priest would ask.

"Her name is María," the parent would answer.

"María," the priest would say, "I bless you in the name of the Father, the Son, and the Holy Spirit."

The priest made the sign of the cross over each child's head as he spoke the traditional blessing. The mother or father would echo the priest's amen before returning to the pew. Sometimes the priest held the child in his arms; other times he whispered brief words of encouragement or congratulation to the parents. Occasionally he might pray briefly for other needs the family or the child might have.

My mother remembers that we were sitting near the back of the sanctuary. Finally it was time for us to move forward to the altar. Mom says the whole church grew quiet as she and Grandma stood to take me forward. Grandma got up out of the pew first, then leaned down and took me from my mother's arms.

The priest moved forward to greet us. He didn't need to ask my name. "José Antonio Melendez Rodriquez," he said, his voice booming through the quiet sanctuary, "I bless you in the name of the Father, the Son, and the Holy Spirit."

Then the priest took me in his arms and held me up proudly before the whole congregation. Mom remembers that he kept me there in the place of honor for twice as long as any other child. He even pinned a beautiful medallion on my blanket, bearing the outline of the Infant Jesus of Prague. He kissed me on the forehead, made the sign of the cross a second time, and prayed a long and moving prayer of blessing just for me.

"You're doing a good thing, the right thing, to bring young Tony to the service," he had told my mother earlier. "Be proud of him," he had instructed her. "Let everybody see how much you love him."

Unfortunately, it was then as it is today. Too often people are embarrassed by handicapped children. To hide the imperfection, parents hide the child. They may love their physically or emotionally disabled son or daughter, but they keep him or her hidden anyway. From the beginning, however, my mother refused to hide me.

When the blessings had ended and the song of benediction had been sung, the parents and their children followed the crucifer, the children's choir, and the priest out of the church and around the plaza in a noisy, happy parade.

My mother and my grandmother both remember marching proudly in that parade. Grandma insisted on carrying me the full route.

"Hello, Mrs. Rodriquez," someone shouted from the crowded sidewalk. "That's a beautiful grandson you have there."

Grandma smiled and held me even closer.

"Hello, Mrs. Melendez," another said, walking into the street to look down at the bundle in my grandmother's arms and then to embrace my proud mother. "Little Tony is very handsome today!"

Dad and Grandpa met us at the front door after our parade through the streets of Rivas and welcomed us with hugs. The day ended well for my whole family, but it had begun poorly for my dad. That morning Mom had found my father sitting alone in their darkened bedroom. He was crying, and it made her angry.

"Why do you cry so much?" she asked him. "God has his reasons. He will give us strength."

Mom is amazing. In those two short sentences she dispensed with everything there was to cry about. Dad was feeling sad for me, trying to comprehend what it would mean to be a child and then a man without arms. But he was also feeling sad for himself, realizing how difficult and complex his life had become. Who could blame him for his tears? Who would fault anyone for weeping at a time like that?

But because of Mom's faith in God, she saw the matter differently. After my mother's first tears, I don't think she ever wept that way again. She refused to feel sad for me; she believed with all her heart that God had a wonderful purpose for my life. She reminded everybody about Jesus' story of the man born blind. When the people asked why he was born that way, Jesus said it was so that the will of God could be done through him.

She refused to feel sad for herself either, or for her husband and family. God had a plan for their lives too. And though my limits might limit each of them, she believed that God had trusted, even honored, them with this responsibility and that he would provide all the strength that they needed to see it through.

THE RED BALLOON

Over the next few months the town opened its heart to me and to my family. By the time Grandpa and Grandma drove me and Mom to our little company house at the edge of Rivas, dozens of gifts had been sent there by relatives, friends, neighbors, and even strangers we had never met.

"Your dad and I sat on the floor of the living room and opened all your presents," Mom recalls. "There were baby clothes and diapers, bottles and blankets, and dozens and dozens of toys."

Just two or three months after I was born, Grandpa Melendez called from El Salvador. "We have to see the baby," he told my dad. "We have to make sure for ourselves that everything will be all right." It was a long journey by air and automobile. My father tried to assure him that there was no reason to worry. Grandpa and Grandma insisted on seeing for themselves and days later they made the journey from San Salvador to Managua. My father's brothers, Pablo and Gilbert, and his sister, Lupe, came, too. Dad picked them up in the airport and drove them half way across Nicaragua to our home in Rivas. Mom remembers that these loving, caring members of our wider family were also bearing toys "for little Tony."

Even with all her faith in my future, my mother couldn't stand that pile of children's toys. My father and José were playing with the little toy cars and trucks, the stuffed cloth rabbit, the plastic dinosaur, and the rubber building blocks. They got more and more excited as each new gift was unwrapped.

Suddenly my mother got up on her knees and began to throw the toys into a large cardboard box.

"What are you doing?" my father asked.

"I'm putting them away," she answered.

"But why put them away?" he asked her. "They're for little Tony."

By that time Mom had cleared the floor of every last toy and she was dragging the heavy box toward the closet. My brother began to cry when Mom stuffed the box of toys into the closet, closed the door, and returned.

"I don't want Tony to see them," she said quietly. "He can't play with them, so why make him feel bad?"

My dad knew enough not to question her decision at the time. He just dried José's tears, nodded at my mother, and waited.

Nobody knows for certain how the large red balloon got into my crib several months later. Mom still thinks Dad put it there. I was less than six months old, so I don't remember the incident; but since everybody else in the family has told me the story in one version or another, I suppose it's true.

"I was in the kitchen," Mom told me, "and I could hear your dad and brother laughing in the bedroom where you had been sleeping in your crib.

"'Sara María,' your father shouted, 'Come! Look!'"

Mom ran into the little bedroom. She could see a bright-red balloon bouncing up and down above the crib, but she couldn't see who was bouncing it. José had climbed up the side of the crib and was balancing on the rail. He wasn't even near the red balloon. And my father was on the other side of the crib with his hands in the air.

"I'm not doing it," he said, laughing aloud.

Mom walked over to the crib, drying her hands on her apron and staring at the bouncing red balloon. She could hear the happy noises I was making. But when she saw why I was making them, she almost broke into tears.

The balloon was drifting down toward the end of the crib. Just as Mom leaned over the crib, I went scooting on my back after it. She watched as I trapped the balloon against the bars of the crib with my clubfoot and then kicked it into the air again with my good foot and ankle. Perhaps the story has grown with the years of telling it, but Mom says I even caught the balloon once with both feet, held it for a second, and then tossed it up into the air again with my eleven little toes.

Dad put his arm around my mother as she stood looking down at me. Nothing was said between them. Mom just watched for a moment and then walked out of the room. Dad and José followed. Mom went directly to the closet where my toys were stored. She opened the door, pulled down the box, and dragged it back into my room. They filled my crib with toys that day. Soon the red balloon was bouncing off little toy cars and trucks, the stuffed rabbit, the plastic dinosaur, and the rubber building blocks.

"After that," my mother said, "I never tried to guess what you could do and what you couldn't. I just let you decide, and you've been surprising me ever since!"

3. The Journey to America

My mother, carrying me in her arms, and my father climbed off the bus from Rivas and walked quickly through Managua's most beautiful park, the Parque Darío. I was about four months old that afternoon as my parents paused for just a moment near the large winged monument to the Nicaraguan poet Rubén Darío. Mom read the inscription on its marble base, while Dad opened a map of the capital and searched it for a street name written on the envelope in his hand.

"Señor," a little voice whispered at his side.

My parents looked down at the eleven- or twelve-year-old girl standing in the shadow of the monument. She was carrying an infant boy who must have been her little brother. The child had only one arm, and that was just a rounded stump without a hand.

"Señor?" the girl whispered again, looking first at my dad and then back at the infant she was holding.

My parents stared at the baby with a growing sense of dread. Other ragged, dirty children were running in their direction. Many of the street urchins were physically or mentally handicapped. All were shouting, "Señor?" All were hoping for a handout. My dad reached into his pocket for some coins, placed them in the little girl's outstretched hand, and hurried my mother and me toward the National Palace and the hospital and medical clinic nearby.

My mother's uncle in Rivas, Dr. Toño, had recommended an orthopedic specialist in Managua to treat my clubfoot. He had written a letter that my father was carrying to the doctor as a letter of introduction. When my parents reached the medical clinic, they presented the letter to the nurse on duty, who asked them to be seated in a rather large, dingy waiting room already crammed with adults and children waiting for medical attention.

As they sat in the crowded clinic, my parents talked about the ragged little girl and her brother with only one arm. Health conditions in Nicaragua were very poor at that time, as they were throughout Central and South America. Contaminated water systems, poor sanitation, and overcrowded housing made matters worse. Diseases such as tuberculosis, tetanus, and typhoid fever were commonplace. There was a serious shortage of doctors, nurses, and trained medical technicians, and even fewer skilled specialists. Hospitals were overcrowded and understaffed; medical equipment was often outdated and in ill-repair.

The infant mortality rate in Nicaragua, though better than many third-world countries, was still 160 deaths to every 1,000 live births. More than one out of every ten children born would die before his or her first birthday. And of those who did survive their first year, many died before their tenth birthday of such childhood diseases as measles, mumps, and chicken pox—diseases that would be easily treated and cured in the United States by a family doctor or even a drugstore pharmacist.

Most of the people in my country were poor. But never forget: poor people—then and now—love their children too. Why is it so easy to forget that mothers and fathers living in the poorest slums of the most desperate cities in the world love their children just as much as rich people living in mansions behind guarded walls?

Unfortunately, however, when the sons and the daughters of the poor get sick, they can't afford a doctor or an emergency hospital, even if one is available. They can't even buy toothpaste and toilet paper, let alone aspirin or penicillin. And poor children who are born handicapped have almost no chance to receive the special medical and psychological care they need. When I was born, the life expectancy in Nicaragua for normal, healthy adults was only fifty-five years. In the past twenty-five years the situation hasn't changed all that much; for handicapped or sickly children, despair and death wait just around the corner.

It isn't that my country has no natural resources. God blessed Nicaragua with rich soil, abundant water, great forests, valuable mineral reserves, including gold, copper, and silver, and adequate deposits of lead, antimony, tungsten, bauxite, marble, and gypsum. But the people are poor because over the centuries Nicaragua's natural wealth has been exploited by a handful of colonial powers and a clique of greedy families who refused to share the wealth. For twenty-five years before my birth, Anastasio Somoza and his family ruled our country with an iron hand. General Somoza had little opposition until 1962, the year I was born, when the Sandinista movement organized in the slums of Managua to wage a guerrilla war against him and his successors.

I am not a political person, but I am tired of tyranny from the right and from the left. While the Contra versus Sandinista debate continues, the children of Nicaragua are caught in the cross-fire—without food, clothing, or housing, let alone education or health care. While the politicians and the revolutionaries fight for power, the little ones of my country (and of the world) go on suffering and dying as before.

As Mom and Dad sat in the clinic waiting room in Managua, they couldn't escape the memories of those beggar children in the park. It's bad enough to be a normal, healthy child in a poor, third-world nation, but a child with no arms was guaranteed an uncertain future at best. They knew that I needed serious medical treatment. They knew too that I would require special schools to help in overcoming my various handicaps. The best place to receive that kind of care was in the United States, 5,000 miles to the north. It was growing more and more obvious to Mom and Dad that they were going to have to make the most difficult decision of their lives.

"Mr. and Mrs. Melendez," the doctor said after examining me that day, "we can remove Tony's extra toe. That surgery wouldn't be difficult. But your son will never walk until he has a series of operations on his clubfoot."

Every two weeks for the next few months my mom and dad took me to the hospital in Managua for checkups and therapy, waiting for the moment surgery could begin. We traveled three hours each way in a van. The roads were often washed out by torrential rains or blocked by fallen boulders or mudslides, and the buses were just too crowded with people and their baggage, boxes, and bicycles. Animals in cages were roped to the roof; some scampered free up and down the aisles.

The bumping up and down and the narrow hairpin curves always made me sick. Mom said that all the other passengers would open their windows when they saw us coming, knowing that just a few miles down the road I would be passing my nausea on to them. Still, back and forth we went, hoping that the doctor could perform the series of operations I needed to walk, waiting for him to arrange for surgical time, a bed in the hospital, and an operating team. The waiting seemed to go on forever. Every time we got to Managua, the doctor announced another delay.

SURGERY IN MANAGUA

Finally, one afternoon in May 1962, my mother took me to the capital alone. The doctor greeted her happily. "Tony will have his surgery at last," he told her.

"When?" she asked him.

"Today," he replied.

"But I brought no extra clothes," she said. "I thought that today would be just another checkup. I planned to take him back to Rivas on the evening bus."

"Someone can bring you clothing," the doctor said, moving my mother toward his office. "Tony must be in surgery immediately."

Mom tried unsuccessfully to reach my father on the telephone. Finally she made contact with Grandpa Rodriquez at his office, and he found Dad at the refinery. When Dad learned that his six-month-old son was going into surgery, he borrowed a car, speeded the three-hour distance to Managua in less than a hundred minutes, and arrived in the surgical waiting room just as I was being wheeled into recovery.

"They cut off his extra toe," Mom told my father, "and they began work on straightening his foot. But it's just a beginning. The doctor says there's much more work to be done. He wonders if we really want to do it here."

Mom remembers waiting for my recovery that day. They were exhausted, physically and emotionally. The trips to Managua had accomplished so very little; they didn't feel confident that they would ever get the medical help I needed to survive. Once again my parents talked about traveling to Los Angeles. There were excellent doctors there, and hospitals. But California seemed so far away. They had no car to drive the 5,000 miles, and no money put away to pay for gas, oil, food, and accommodations along the way. Neither of them could speak English. But Dad couldn't shake the memories of the children and adults who begged for money on the streets of Managua.

"Tony will *not* end up a beggar," my father whispered to himself. "Whatever it takes, Tony will get the medical help he needs—and an education to go with it."

They saw me several hours later, lying in a hospital crib with a cast on my left leg. For two days they watched and waited in my hospital room. By the time we headed home, the anesthetic had worn off and my leg had begun to hurt. By the time we arrived in Rivas, my leg was itching and burning painfully. I had no hands to scratch with, of course, so that first night at home, lying in my crib, I rubbed the cast against the bars of my crib, hoping to stop the pain. Unfortunately, I rubbed so hard and so long that the plaster gave way and the cast fell off. My parents had to take the next available bus back to Managua.

The doctor, amazed, put on a new cast. In twenty-four hours I had twisted and rubbed it off again! Back and forth we went, the ordeal taxing my parents' love and the doctor's good will. And he hadn't even begun the *serious* surgery on my clubfoot.

"What will we do?" my mother asked one night. "Tony needs more help than he's getting here. And when the leg heals and is straight, he'll need special therapy to learn to walk. He'll need false arms, and he'll have to attend special schools to learn to use them."

My parents prayed and waited for a sign. Mother went to church every morning to pray for guidance, while Dad paced up and down the cane fields or hiked deep into the jungle thinking about what had to be done.

THE LUCKY NUMBERS

"Buy your tickets now," the old lottery vendor shouted above the noise of the workers leaving the hospital where Grandpa worked as chief accountant.

"I'll buy one," Grandpa said, "for my grandson Tony."

The vendor smiled at Grandpa and reached to the bottom of the stack of blue-and-red tickets.

"This one is for Tony," he said. "May God bring you good luck, Rodriquez!"

Dad and Grandpa had decided to pool their cash with friends at work to buy a chance at winning the national lottery. My mother and grandmother teased them about their "big gamble" until the notice was posted that their number had won. Dad's share of the prize was the equivalent of $5,000!

"We'll buy a used car," my folks decided. "It will make the trips to Managua so much easier."

They didn't share their dream of driving to America—not yet. They bought a 1956 four-door Chevrolet Bel Air with 65,000 miles on it. It was dented and rusty, and the vinyl seats were worn; but the engine ran perfectly. After waxing and rubbing that old two-tone green relic until it shone, Mom and Dad drove me proudly to the clinic in Managua. Mom remembers how Dad honked and waved happily as they passed the old bus chugging up the road to the capital, loaded down with people and their baggage.

"This car would make it to California," he said as they pulled up before their little cottage on the refinery grounds in Rivas after the return trip late that night. "We could do it."

My mother had three sisters living in Los Angeles. She wrote them to inquire about doctors and hospitals in southern California. They wrote back excitedly inviting Mom and Dad to stay with them while I was being treated. Some of the Melendez family had also migrated to southern California. My father's three aunts had good jobs and comfortable homes in an old neighborhood in east Los Angeles. They heard about my medical needs and added their invitation to the others. When my mother's sister wrote from east Los Angeles inviting the family to her wedding, my dad felt ready at last to share his plan.

"We'll *all* go," my grandpa announced at the table that night.

"All of us," my mother groaned, "in that one car?"

"Sure, why not?" Grandpa answered.

And with that, it was settled. My parents marked a map with the route we would follow: Dad would drive us up the west coast of Nicaragua, through Managua and León. The unfinished Intercontinental Highway would take us across the southern tip of Honduras and into El Salvador. We would drive to San Salvador, the capital, and stay with my father's folks for a few days en route. Then we would pass through Guatemala on Highway 190 on our way to Mexico City. From Mexico City it was just 3,000 miles more to San Diego, where my mother's sister Muriel and her fiancé would meet us and help us make the crossing into the United States of America.

Dad and Grandpa tuned the engine of the old Chevrolet. Mom and Grandma packed dried fruit and meat, corn tortillas wrapped in tinfoil, plastic bottles of water, a medicine chest, an emergency repair kit, spare clothing, bathing suits, towels, blankets, and cardboard boxes filled with necessary provisions.

The whole family was going: Mom and Dad, José, Grandpa and Grandma Rodriquez, and their four youngest boys. Ten of us squeezed ourselves, our baggage, and our provisions for the weeklong, 5,000-mile journey into that ancient Chevrolet. The family said goodbye to neighbors and friends, promising that we would return when I had finished my surgery and was well on my way to recuperation. We began the journey late in December 1962. My parents planned that we would be in northern Mexico, if not in California, on my first birthday.

MCDONALD'S GOLDEN ARCHES

Obviously I remember nothing of that first long trip across Central America. And Mom is still trying to forget it. The trip took seventeen days instead of the planned seven. Somewhere along the route I picked up a bad case of dysentery, and in Mexico I almost died from it. In a little village near Durango, in the middle of the night, I became feverish and began to convulse. My dad woke half the town trying to find a doctor. Once located, the doctor took one look at me and shook his head.

"You can pray for him," he advised, "and I'll fill him with antibiotics, but there's little hope that your son will survive."

All through that night and the next day, my parents and grandparents stood vigil. They wrapped me in cool, damp towels to lower the fever. And they prayed. In twenty-four hours the fever broke; my normal color returned. The doctor was amazed and sent us on our way.

When we finally reached the United States, the immigration officials signaled us quickly through: we had relatives in Los Angeles, and we were coming only for a medical visit. The border-crossing was easy, almost anticlimactic, after such a trip.

Aunt Muriel and her fiancé, René, were waiting for our arrival on the California side of the Mexico border. René remembers how we looked that day after almost 384 hours on the hot, dusty highways of Central America and Mexico.

"The windows were black," he said. "The dust and mud were caked so thick on the panes that you couldn't even see through them. The tires were so low that they looked like four rolling flats. Your dad was too exhausted to get out; he just rolled down the window and stared up at me. His face was streaked with dust and sweat. The car was filled with people draped across each other like victims of a terrible accident."

Apparently Muriel and René washed off the family in the restroom of a Texaco station, herded us into a McDonald's restaurant near the border, bought everybody Big Macs, french fries, and milkshakes, and watched as the family revived.

"Welcome to America," he said. "Too bad there's no Statue of Liberty here to greet you."

Actually, the cool shade of McDonald's golden arches wasn't a bad place to begin our visit to the Promised Land. I just wish I could remember that day. But I was just one year and seven days old.

Mom said that as my father sat in the restaurant eating his Big Mac and fries, his eyes filled with tears. "I wonder if we'll ever go back home," he said to no one in particular. Mom took his hand in hers and held it as she spooned me my first taste of a strawberry shake.

4. New Life in America

The freeway from San Diego to Los Angeles was twelve lanes wide, or so Mom remembers. And on that Sunday afternoon as we followed Aunt Muriel's car toward the final stop on our seventeen-day trip across Central America and Mexico, the traffic was bumper to bumper.

"It's the racing crowd from Del Mar," Muriel's fiancé explained, "and the tourists from Tijuana and San Diego heading home. You just have to grin and bear it."

For four hours we inched toward our temporary new home in L.A. They say that I lay in my mother's arms and slept the entire way, but my dad and mom, my grandpa and grandma, and the older children all remember just staring out the window, silently watching the endless flow of trucks, station wagons, campers, old cars, new cars, and limousines all flowing toward the city.

It was early evening when we arrived at the little rental house in east Los Angeles where three of Mom's sisters lived. They came rushing out the front door and into the street to greet us. Food and drink were ready and waiting on a rough picnic table in the back yard, and friends and neighbors gathered to welcome the Rodriquez-Melendez clan. As Mom remembers it, everyone wanted to pick me up, hold me, and offer words of encouragement to my parents on the hospitals and doctors in Los Angeles.

Late into the night the family reminisced about Rivas, the beach-house at Lake Nicaragua, vacations on the sea at the port of San Juan del Sur, and the green and mysterious jungles that had been the family playground when they too were children. My dad must have been exhausted after his 5,000-mile journey, but long after the sun had set and the neighbors had retired, Dad had the whole family laughing at his stories about Melendez the crocodile in Rivas's well, the boa constrictor Mom discovered in her bathtub, and the irreverent parrot Dad tried to teach to say amen but instead swore like a sailor when the priest came to visit.

Dad found his guitar at the bottom of the pile of baggage in the station wagon and produced it to a flurry of applause. My father was a good singer with a rich baritone voice. He accompanied himself on his guitar with a wonderful mixture of classic and native styles. The guitar trio Dad formed in Rivas had had several opportunities to travel and record, but he preferred to sing for his family and for fun. That night, after a few beers, Dad led the family as they harmonized on the songs of Nicaragua and of home.

> "Salve a ti, Nicaragua! En tu suelo
> Ya no ruge la voz del cañón
> Ni se tiñe con sangre de hermanos
> Tu glorioso pendón bicolor.
>
> Brille hermosa la paz en tu cielo,
> Nada empane tu gloria inmortal,
> Que el trabajo es tu digno laurel
> Y el honor es tu ensena triunfal."

In English, the song goes like this:

> Here's to you, Nicaragua!
> In your land, the voice of the cannon does not roar.
> Neither is your flag tainted with the blood of
> your brothers.
>
> Peace shines brightly in your heavens.
> Nothing stops your immortal glory,
> which is the result of your noble work,
> and honor is your triumphant goal.

One by one the children fell asleep in the arms of their parents or with their heads cradled on the hard wooden table. Wrapped in a light blanket, I slept in my mother's arms for the entire evening.

Mom still isn't sure how we all fit into her aunts' home that night. There were three little bedrooms in that old wood-framed house on Green Street. There was no extra room in the inn when we arrived, yet we were greeted with open arms. We were family;

we were in need. And regardless of the discomfort or inconvenience that our presence caused, we were welcome. Looking back on that first night in America makes me proud of my roots in a culture deeply committed to family and to the ancient Christian value of hospitality.

My mother's Grandmother Valdez shared her tiny bedroom with Mom's three aunts: Dolores and Conchita Valdez and Engracia Mimi Sandoval. Grandpa and Grandma Rodriquez were given the second bedroom to share with their four youngest children; Mom, Dad, José, and I slept in the small attic-bedroom; while Mom's sister Muriel and Mimi's three children slept on sleeping bags on the floor of the living room. There were approximately twenty of us spread throughout the house that first night, and at least thirteen of us lived together (as my mom remembers it) without even a cross word or an argument in the long months that followed.

DISCOVERING THE NEW WORLD

Dad awakened first that next morning and went for a walk by himself to scout the city. In 1963 the streets of east Los Angeles were already crowded with Hispanic immigrants from Mexico and Central and South America. With over one million men, women, and children of Hispanic heritage, Los Angeles had the seventh-largest Spanish-speaking community in the world.

The main streets of Los Angeles, from west to east, were already crowded with taco stands, liquor stores, gas stations and garages, endless weary little shops, fast-food outlets, fortune tellers, and tarot-card readers, interspersed with an occasional storefront church, law office, or public service agency. Already the struggle against gangs and graffiti had begun. And early in the morning certain corners were crowded with men hoping to be hired for a day-laborer job. Sidewalk vendors wandering up and down the streets with carts sold native products, home-cooked ethnic foods, or ice-cream. All during the day and night police cars, ambulances, and fire trucks raced through the neighborhoods, their sirens screaming.

There were no parks or playgrounds near my aunts' home—at least none that my mother can remember. My dad didn't even discover *any* green on his first venture out into east Los Angeles. "There are no trees," he told my mother later that morning. "The lawns are brown, there are no flowers growing around the houses, and the flatness goes on forever."

Dad walked for miles—hoping, I suppose, to find something that could replace the green fields and cool, shaded jungles of Rivas. But the jungle of black asphalt and gray cement that was east Los Angeles left him feeling homesick and lost.

"In spite of the way he was feeling about leaving Nicaragua," Mom told me, "on that very first day your father made a list of his priorities. He needed to get you to the doctor; that was the first and most important item on his list. Second, he needed a job to earn money to pay your medical bills, to buy food for the family, and to find us a little place of our own to rent. Third, he needed a green card to be employed legally in this country. And fourth, he wanted to be relicensed, here in America, in his own area of expertise, so that he could find a meaningful position and not be limited to streetcorner job marts."

Dad didn't want charity. He hadn't come to America looking for a handout from the government, from his family, or from his friends. He was educated in agriculture and animal husbandry, and he had experience in farming and management at the sugar-cane refinery in Rivas. A professional, he was willing and ready to work hard to pay his bills.

Before our first full day in Los Angeles had ended, Dad had found the orthopedic specialist recommended to him by the clinic in Managua and made an appointment for the doctor to see me later that week. He had also found a lawyer who would help him get a green card (and in fact got one before thirty days had passed). And he found a job in a sweat shop on the second floor of an old building in downtown Los Angeles.

"They made children's clothes there," Mom remembers. "There seemed to be floors and floors of women sewing at their own sewing machines. They were paid not a salary or by the hour, but for every garment they produced. And because every piece-work employee was as desperate as your father to survive, the women stayed bent over their machines from sunrise to sunset."

The owner was a strange little man who walked up and down the aisles mumbling to himself and staring down at the workers. Occasionally he would grab a piece of an unfinished garment, pull it from the poor worker's machine, and hold it up for all to see, pointing out a missed stitch or an uneven seam. He would end his tirade with angry shouts and curses, threatening to fire the worker.

My father was hired to sweep up the scraps of cloth, to help fix the sewing machines when they malfunctioned, and generally to keep the sweat shop in order. On his first day one of the women came out of the one restroom and shouted at him across the room.

"Hey, Mexican," she yelled, "what's the matter with you? This toilet is filthy. Clean it up!"

Mom says that my father stood there in shock. Dad didn't know many English words, but the angry voice and gestures were perfectly clear to him. Slowly he turned to face the woman who had yelled at him. For a moment the sewing machines stopped. The room grew unnaturally quiet as the women all looked impatiently in Dad's direction. Still he didn't move: he was a proud man, and he had been shamed. As he stood there struggling to overcome his anger, a chorus of voices added their own complaints about "the dirty joint" before the boss walked in and silenced them.

"The toilet brush is under the john, Melendez," the boss yelled at my father as he left the room. "Use it good!"

My father spoke little English, but it was pretty obvious what was being asked of him. Dad was an educated man. His employees at the refinery in Rivas had called him "sir" and "Mr. Melendez." No one had ever cursed him or ordered him about on the job. And he had certainly never cleaned a public toilet in his life.

Mom remembers how my father looked that night when he returned from his first day on the job in America. "He tried to smile at me," she recalled, "but his eyes didn't sparkle as before. He said the job went *suficiente bien.* But his shoulders were stooped and his voice cracked. When I held him in my arms, he hugged me halfheartedly and walked quickly from the room."

By morning Dad seemed to have recovered. He had cleaned their toilets and had taken their abuse for the minimum wage, $1.25 an hour. But he wouldn't suffer their indignities forever. That same week he began English lessons, and immediately he started his search for a second full-time job. By Friday he had been hired as a weekend replacement to mow lawns with a large gardening crew. For the next several months he worked ten or twelve hours a weekday in the sweat shop and ten to twelve hours a day on Saturday and Sunday, pushing a lawnmower and trimming hedges.

On their very first Saturday in America, Dad and Mom took me to the orthopedic specialist. The doctor examined me; X-rays were taken; my parents were interviewed. Then, after several weeks of waiting, they returned me to the doctor for his diagnosis.

"Your son won't walk," the doctor explained, "until his clubfoot is surgically straightened. That goal will require a series of operations and long-term therapy and retraining."

The doctor outlined the costs and asked Mom and Dad about their medical insurance. They had none. He asked about money that they might have put away. Again they shook their heads sadly. It was plain to both my parents that they couldn't afford the costs of my surgeries without financial assistance. My mother remembers that long ride home—and the growing disappointment, anger, and frustration that she could see in my father's eyes. He had traveled 5,000 miles to get the medical attention I needed, only to discover upon his arrival in America that he couldn't afford it.

Even as long and hard as Dad was working, at $1.25 an hour he could hardly pay for rent, utilities, food, clothing, and transportation—let alone bills for doctors, hospitals, therapy technicians, and medical equipment. To complicate matters further, just after our arrival in America, Mom discovered that she was pregnant. The anticipation of more medical bills and another child to feed, clothe, and house added to Dad's growing desperation about money.

A MOMENT OF HOPE

About that time, in a Spanish-language newspaper, my father read about a graduate program offered at Cal Poly University, at the eastern edge of the city. Apparently they offered classes certifying agricultural specialists who had been trained and degreed in other countries. The university promised on-the-job training and eventually a good job on a produce farm or with a landscape firm.

My father took a day off from his work at the garment shop, drove to Pomona, found the university registrar's office, and applied. A Spanish-speaking administrator interviewed Dad, and after almost an hour with him assured him that within a very short time he could be certified in this country.

Mom remembers how he took her in his arms that night and practically wept with excitement. He began to hope again. One week later he repeated the long drive back across the city to keep his appointment with his academic counselor at Cal Poly.

"I'm sorry, Mr. Melendez," the man began, looking rather embarrassed. "You qualify for the program except in one detail: you aren't a citizen. The certification program is for citizens only."

My father was stunned. He thanked the counselor and headed blindly for the door.

"Of course, Mr. Melendez," the man added, "if you become a citizen, we could reconsider you for the program."

My father had come to America to find medical help for me. He hadn't planned on moving here or on becoming a United States citizen. He loved Nicaragua. He thought that after the two or three years of medical treatment that I needed, he and our family would return to Central America. But without a good job, he couldn't pay for the medical care. And I would never walk without those operations.

So Dad enrolled in night-school English classes and in a neighborhood seminar that led to citizenship. He continued working ten to twelve hours a day, but he quit his weekend gardening to study English and to prepare himself to become a citizen of the United States.

Dad and Mom were saving every dime they could to pay for my first surgery, scheduled for December 1963. All the family were trying to help raise the funds as well. Grandpa Rodriquez had even volunteered to stay in America, get a job, and contribute his income toward my surgeries. But Grandpa, a trained accountant and a skilled and honored administrator for the hospital in Rivas, could find in America only jobs washing dishes or sweeping floors. Grandma also wanted to help: she volunteered to take care of me after my operations. But both grandparents soon realized that they could only add to the burden here. Mom remembers the tearful night when Grandpa and Grandma Rodriquez said goodbye.

We had lived six months crowded into the little home of my mother's three sisters in east Los Angeles. They had shared their house without complaint, and they had helped provide food and clothing for the family as well. My father was embarrassed to be causing them so much inconvenience, however. When he had saved enough money, he rented a little apartment for our family on nearby Mott Street.

Our first family home in America had just one bedroom, a small living room, and a kitchen. Mom and Dad used the bedroom, and José and I slept in the living room. It was a tiny place, Mom remembers, but after sharing one bathroom with twelve other people for six long months, she thought our little apartment seemed like a castle.

My sister Mayella was born on October 11, 1964, soon after we moved. Dad spent the mornings and early afternoons taking Mom and me to the doctor, and he worked all night to pay our expenses. Still, with the doctor and maternity-ward bills, once again the family resources ran dry. And my first surgery was scheduled for early in December—just weeks away.

A GIFT OF LOVE

"Mr. Melendez," my doctor said, "I have some very good news for you."

Because my dad had no money, he had gone to the surgeon's office to see if some arrangement could be made to postpone payment for the imminent operation. The doctor smiled broadly and shook Dad's hand.

"Have you heard of the March of Dimes?" he said.

My father waited for a translator to translate.

"No," he answered. "What is it?"

"That's a long story," the doctor answered, "but to make it short, it's an organization of good and generous people working to treat and prevent birth defects in children. I thought that they might help you and little Tony, so I wrote a few letters and made a few phone calls. One of their representatives visited me today. I showed her Tony's X-rays and asked her what the March of Dimes might do to help you and your son."

As the doctor's long speech in English continued, Dad waited desperately for the translation. The translator smiled politely but said nothing. Dad grew more and more confused. Finally the translator turned to my father, put his hands on his shoulders, and began to speak.

"The March of Dimes will be responsible for Tony's operations," he said quietly. "Señor, they are going to pay for everything!"

My mother was waiting at home. Her heart was filled with fear: if Dad's mission failed, perhaps her son would never walk. After what seemed like days, she saw her husband climb out of the car and race up the walkway. He threw open the door, took Mom in his arms, and swung her about the room.

Mom remembers pouring coffee for Dad and then sitting at the kitchen table beside him as he told her about the miracle of the March of Dimes. They both cried that day. Mom remembers her heart just running over with gratitude to all those people she didn't know who cared enough about her son to pay the bills that would help me walk for the very first time.

"Mama," she said over the static of the long-distance line reaching all the way to Rivas, Nicaragua, "the March of Dimes is going to pay for all the operations. The next time you see your little Tony, he'll be walking!"

Because neither Mom nor Dad had known anything about the March of Dimes, the doctor had given them a pamphlet in Spanish describing the organization and its history of good works. And he seemed confident that Mom and Dad could trust the March of

Dimes to deliver what it had promised. Slowly, tears running down their cheeks, Mom and Dad read about the March of Dimes, established in 1938 by President Franklin D. Roosevelt as the National Foundation for Infantile Paralysis. Comedian Eddie Cantor gave the foundation its new name, the National Foundation–March of Dimes, because it raised its funds from donors ten cents at a time.

In its first twenty years of operation, the March of Dimes had helped fund research for a vaccine that could kill the polio virus that was crippling tens of thousands of children around the world; and they had provided medical treatment, physical therapy, and iron lungs for polio victims. While helping to eliminate polio, the March of Dimes had also sponsored research into a cure for sickle-cell anemia, rubella, tuberculosis, and dozens of other crippling and fatal childhood diseases.

By 1958 the March of Dimes had expanded its original goal to include completely eliminating the birth defects that still cripple newborn children in every nation in the world. This year, in America alone, birth defects will strike 250,000 infants. About 15 million American adults and children now have defects and deformities suffered at birth, with 1.2 million of them hospitalized every year for treatment. Sixty thousand Americans of all ages die every year as the result of birth defects. Illnesses or deformities received at birth are the nation's most serious children's health problem and consume billions of dollars yearly in medical care costs.

That day my mother and father learned how much the March of Dimes had accomplished on behalf of the world's suffering children. And over the weeks and months that followed, they would learn firsthand how much the March of Dimes would care for me. Without the help of this generous organization, Mom and Dad couldn't have paid for the series of operations that I needed. But because of their generosity to a tiny crippled baby from Nicaragua, I can walk, run, and play the guitar today.

I was admitted for surgery at Orthopaedic Hospital in Los Angeles just a few weeks before Christmas of 1963. The surgeons there broke and reset certain bones in my lower left leg and twisted ankle. Mom remembers looking down on me, swathed in white plaster and crying out in pain, in the recovery room.

Mom and Dad visited me every day during my long hospital recuperation. They drove across Los Angeles, when the car ran, or borrowed Tarcisio's or René's car to make the journey. Mom told me that Dad always sneaked brightly wrapped candies into the room for me. She remembers how he leaned over my bed and whispered words of encouragement or sang to me when I cried. She told me that often his tears would mingle with mine as he bent down over me, trying to love my pain away.

I was almost two years old (and we had been in this country almost a year), but I remember nothing of that first surgery or the weeks of recuperation that followed. My mother, however, recalls in detail that Christmas Eve when I was discharged from the hospital at last and placed into her arms again.

My left leg was in a heavy plaster cast that I kicked and rubbed with my right leg even as Mom carried me from the hospital to my father's waiting car. As my parents drove silently across the city, crowds of shoppers filled the downtown streets and outlying shopping malls, searching for last-minute gifts. Dad and Mom had no money for presents that year, however. Even with the help of the March of Dimes, Dad was barely staying ahead of all the family expenses.

But my parents felt the Christmas spirit. Although evergreen boughs and holly aren't exactly a Central American tradition, Mom and Dad had our little apartment smelling of sap and green branches, candle wax and Christmas cookies. And Dad, who hated plastic trees, had found a discarded evergreen in the back of a large vacant lot where Christmas trees were being sold.

"On Christmas Eve I told the family that you children were our presents that year," Mom remembers. "Mayella was just a few months old, and you were just hours back from the hospital. So I told José Jr. that we didn't need presents—that we could consider Tony and Mayella our gifts."

Once again, our loving family surprised us with their thoughtfulness. Early in the day they began to arrive unexpectedly bearing

My mom is pictured here as a member of the queens court in the International Agricultural Exposition parade in her hometown of Rivas, Nicaragua.

Mom and Dad as a young couple in love (1961).

Mom and Dad on their wedding day, March 5, 1960.

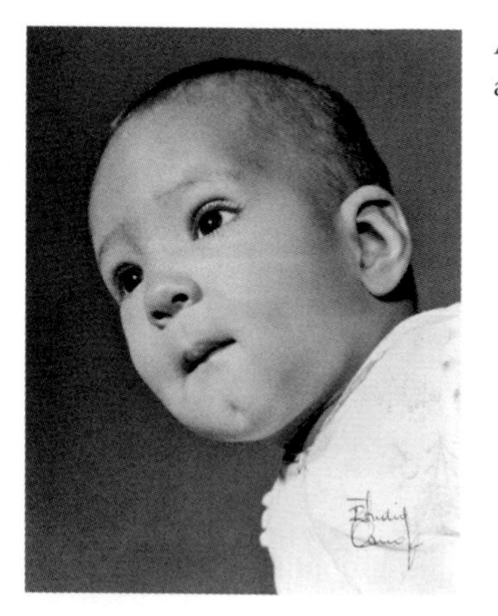

A picture taken in Nicaragua
at five months old.

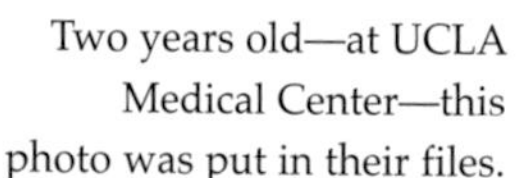

Two years old—at UCLA
Medical Center—this
photo was put in their files.

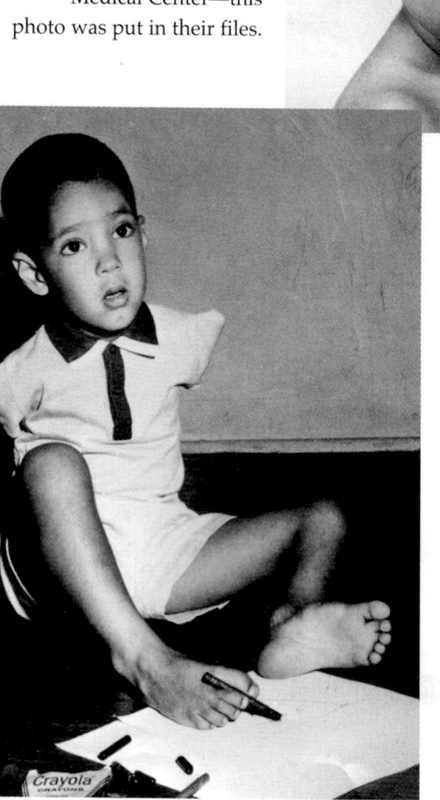

Here I am posing
for a March of Dimes
drawing contest
I had won.

At the age of four, working hard—or should I say playing hard!

The Melendez family together: José, Dad, Mayella, Mom, Mary Lou and me.

Playing on the bed with our toys (cousin, Rene Mandes, José and me).

A trip to the doctor's office with Dad.

At home in Chino, California, enjoying a summer day with family and friends.

Mowing the yard on a hot summer evening.

"I have to kiss him." Next thing I knew the Pope jumped into the audience and kissed me.

In Rome, the Pope reaches to greet me, two years after our encounter in Los Angeles.

Backstage, Jerry Lewis takes a break to meet me, a guest on the MDA telethon.

Chuck Yeager poses with the Melendez brothers at the Super Bowl XXIII NFL Alumni Association banquet, Miami.

José coming up to share some words at a concert in Michigan.

Violeta Chamorro, the President of Nicaragua welcomes me home to my birthplace.

Lou Gosset, Jr. and me conversing after the filming of the Very Special Arts benefit.

The late Jim Hensen, creator of The Muppets, and Kermit the Frog sharing a humorous moment with me.

Rehearsing a song with Crystal Gayle for a Very Special Arts televised benefit, Kennedy Center, Washington, D.C.

Lynn and me at our wedding reception, August 18, 1990.

My daughter Marisa giving me a hug as she and my wife Lynn are introduced by me at a concert.

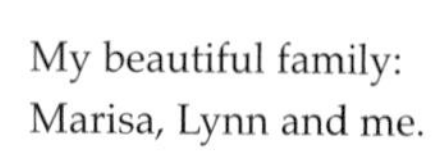

My beautiful family: Marisa, Lynn and me.

gifts. No one in our family was wealthy. Like us most of them had recently migrated from Central America. They were working hard to pay the rent, buy groceries, and pay taxes. Still, they were willing to share what little they had with us.

My mother's cousin, Alma, was the first to arrive early that brisk, Christmas Eve day. Mom still remembers that her arms were filled with gifts. "For José and little Tony," she said. "She even brought us a little Christmas tree," Mom recalls. "It was already decorated. And under her little tree she placed tiny little cars for you two boys, all wrapped in shiny paper, and a tin of fresh baked Christmas cookies."

Apparently, Alma had just left our little apartment when Mom's three aunts arrived. "They looked like the three wisemen," Mom recalls smiling. "They stood at that door with more presents for you boys." Those three generous ladies who had opened their home and their hearts to us brought a box of traditional Central American holiday foods, presents for Mom, Dad, and Mayella, and a tricycle for José and a tiny little pedal fire truck for me.

During that entire day, family and friends arrived bearing more surprises. Mom still remembers the laughter, the tears, and the growing sense of love and gratitude she felt that day. Uncles and aunts, cousins, nephews and nieces all dropped by to wish us Merry Christmas and to make sure that there was food on the table and gifts under the tree.

Mom remembers waking up on Christmas morning to the sound of José Jr.'s laughter. She and Dad tiptoed into the living room to see what was happening. José had awakened early and organized his own party around the Christmas tree. He had managed to carry Mayella into the living room and place her under the tree, and had propped me (in my heavy cast) up beside her. We were draped in ribbons, and four-year-old José was giggling with delight and feeding—or trying to feed—Christmas cookies to both of us.

5. Learning to Walk

Mom says that I began to cry the moment the nurse took my bare foot in her hand. It was my second birthday: January 9, 1964. Almost three weeks had passed since that first surgery in the children's wing of Orthopaedic Hospital in Los Angeles. The bandages had been unwrapped and the stitches removed. Now a technician shot a new set of X-rays and bathed my foot with a green disinfectant soap. After the surgery on my lower leg, it was time to begin the long, uncomfortable process of straightening my clubfoot.

The process was simple. A doctor wrapped my foot, ankle, and calf in soft, thick paper that would protect my skin. Then he slowly forced the foot and ankle into a semblance of the position they should have taken at birth. Gently the doctor pulled my foot downward, bending the stiff ankle to its limit. Then, as he held ankle and foot in place, he wrapped them in bandages permeated with dry plaster of Paris. With the doctor still holding the foot and ankle in place, a nurse brushed the plaster-of-Paris bandages with warm water until they became like wet papier-mâché. The toe-to-knee cast dried quickly, and in just a few minutes I was back in my mother's arms.

Mom remembers how I lay on my back with the cast in the air, kicking it against the bars of my crib to try to break it and regain my freedom. With no arms, and with one leg in a cast, I had just one leg to exercise. Friends and family often remind me of those days, and of the many tricky ways I learned to get along with just that one working leg.

I used the good right leg to play with my stuffed animals, to inch my way along the floor, to keep a balloon in the air, to turn myself over in my crib, and to pound against the wooden bars when I wanted attention. Best of all, Dad used to grab my one good foot and tickle it until I laughed so hard I cried.

A VISIT HOME

Because Dad worked day and night, we didn't see him often in those early years in Los Angeles; but when we did see him, he always brought excitement into our lives. Although the March of Dimes was paying all of my medical bills, Dad still had to work terribly hard just to pay the rest of the family expenses. Every month, however, he tried to put some small amount into a savings account, and slowly that amount grew. Dad had grown terribly homesick, so during the summer of 1964 he announced to the family that we were going back to Central America to visit our friends and family.

We had been in the United States just sixteen months. My club-foot was beginning to straighten, but I still couldn't walk. Every four weeks the doctor would break off the old cast, clean and disinfect the foot, and then straighten it even farther. Then once again bandages would be wrapped and a cast formed. As soon as I got one cast off, another was set in place.

The process had at least six months to go when Dad's patience ran out. He missed the lush green landscape of his homeland; he longed for the lake and the sea. Early in our stay in America, Dad had realized that only in the United States could I have the medical treatment I needed for my foot and the mechanical arms and the training to use them that everyone thought I would need to survive. But my father loved Rivas. East Los Angeles and its environs were crippling his spirit. So Dad began to dream about living six months of each year in Central America and six months in the United States. That way I could be treated and trained by the best doctors available, and yet he could still be refreshed and renewed by the other world he knew and loved best.

In the meantime, my father needed a summer visit to Central America to make it through the long years ahead. When he had saved enough money, he bought an old Plymouth station wagon, tuned the engine himself, and then repaired the tires and replaced the belts. He attached an extra gas tank from a war-surplus jeep and put a heavy rack on top to carry all our baggage.

Mom was equally excited about a visit to Central America to see her friends and family. From the beginning she had used her spare time to sell Amway products to her friends. Before our trip, she used every dollar she had saved from that business to buy consumer items that weren't readily available in Nicaragua or El Salvador: she bought an inexpensive portable stereo, some audio-tapes with popular hit tunes, kitchen supplies, and even beauty products and deodorants. She stuffed every corner of that already loaded wagon with products that she might sell or trade along the way.

At first my dad was skeptical. He didn't want to be arrested at the border for importing goods illegally. "They'll think we're smugglers," he moaned.

"They'll think it's all mine," Mom answered, "or presents for our relatives."

Finally Dad relented, and it was a good thing that he did. Profits from Mom's little import business helped pay our expenses on the trip. After Grandpa and Grandma Rodriquez heard that Dad and Mom were planning a visit to Nicaragua, they dipped into their own small savings account and sent money to help finance the trip. Toward the end of summer, with a few hundred dollars in hand, Dad quit his jobs with the promise that upon his return he would be rehired for each of them. He loaded us all into the station wagon and began the 5,000-mile drive to Rivas.

I was two and a half years old, and my fourth cast was still in place. I lay on the back seat with only one good leg to balance me as we jolted down the Pan American Highway through Mexico, Guatemala, El Salvador, Honduras, and Nicaragua. My dad was so excited about getting home that he seldom stopped even to take a nap along the dusty, washed-out roads we traveled. We stopped to rest in Dad's parents' home in San Salvador, but that was the only real stop we made along the hot, exhausting route. After a short visit we were on the road again. Dad loved his parents and his country, but his heart was in Rivas and in Nicaragua's jungles, rivers, and streams, and in its estuaries filled with wild animals and shaded by great trees and thick green vines.

When we arrived in Rivas, Dad greeted everyone enthusiastically and then disappeared into the countryside. On several subsequent mornings he took long walks in the sugar-cane fields near the refinery, greeting the workers by name and receiving their warm welcome in return. Often he carried José on his shoulders or me or Mayella in his arms. As he walked, he talked to each of us about the trees and flowers we saw along the way. He knew both their technical and popular names; he knew their history and their function in the forest.

In the jungle shade Dad would pause, and placing his finger to his lips for silence, he would point in the direction of a spotted deer or a beautiful, brightly colored parrot. He made up pet names for each of them, told us what they ate and how they lived, and explained why they were important in the balance of nature.

Dad took us to Lake Nicaragua and insisted, against my mom's protests, that we were ready to swim. He tried to put my right leg in the water while keeping my cast clean and dry. He sat me on a towel and built me castles in the sand. He carried me on long walks down the beaches and talked about the volcano that had erupted, trapping the sea in a giant inland lake, and about the sharks and swordfish that had learned to survive in their new freshwater home.

At night my mom and dad gathered with their friends. Dad played his guitar and sang with the members of his old trio. The crowd of old *amigos* sat around the fireplace drinking and talking, laughing and singing until the dark, star-studded sky grew gray and the sun began to rise above Rivas.

After a few weeks in Nicaragua, Dad took me to see our old doctor in Managua. He removed the old cast, examined my foot, and set it carefully in another plaster cast. Dad had explained his two-country plan to the doctor in America, who didn't really like the idea of biyearly absences, or even of our summer trip. He grew even more concerned during our absence, afraid that the foot might not straighten correctly if the process was interrupted—even if I continued regular doctor visits in Nicaragua. We had only been in my grandparents' home for several weeks when Mom's sisters began to call us from the States, urging us to return.

"The doctor wants to see little Tony," my aunt shouted over the long-distance line. "He said you mustn't stay away too long. It's time for Tony to learn to walk."

My father hated the idea of returning to Los Angeles, but he was the first to volunteer. Mom, who was pregnant again and had been nauseated on the journey south, wasn't really ready to return; but Grandpa and Grandma Rodriquez were glad to help her babysit José and Mayella. Another good reason for Dad and me to travel alone: the Plymouth had collapsed upon our arrival in Rivas and was now home to a family of goats in an empty lot on the edge of town.

Dad kissed Mom and the family goodbye, took me in his arms, and caught the bus to Managua, where he bought an airline ticket with money Grandpa had given him. This time the 5,000 miles were covered in one easy day. Twenty-four hours later my father delivered me to Orthopaedic Hospital.

They tell me that the doctor was relieved to see us. He removed the cast, inspected my foot, and decided to begin training me to walk on it immediately. Already there were seven scars reaching from above my ankle down to my toes. A therapist oiled and massaged my rigid ankle and my bent and scarred left foot; then he stood me up on soft mats and encouraged me to take my first solo journey. I sat back down and refused to budge.

Twice a week my father had to take me on the bus across Los Angeles from Inglewood, where we were living with Aunt Muriel, to Orthopaedic Hospital. And twice a week the therapists massaged my foot, then held me around the waist and walked me up and down the mats. Still I wouldn't try walking on my own, however. My left leg was so much shorter than my right that I couldn't balance, and my foot hurt when I placed weight on it.

Right in the middle of my therapy, the buses went on strike, so we moved in with Uncle Tarcisio to be within walking distance of the hospital. My father was determined that I would walk before Mom flew back from Nicaragua. He wanted to surprise her. His plan was simple: the moment Mom got off the plane she would see me toddling down the concourse in her direction.

But there was much to be done before my mother's arrival. We had moved out of our rental house just before our trip to Central America, so upon our return my father had to find another place for the family to live. He left me with Aunt Muriel during the days it took to find an apartment for our family. Finally he found a second-story two-bedroom rental close to Aunt Muriel in Inglewood. Because the neighborhood was near the Los Angeles airport, with noisy planes passing almost constantly overhead, apartments rented cheaply. In the next few days Dad retrieved from storage our Salvation Army and Goodwill chairs, tables, and beds, and our large green-velvet sofa.

THE FIRST STEP ON MY JOURNEY

When my walking lessons at the hospital went too slowly, Dad worked hard to teach me himself. Friends of the family have told me that Dad didn't have an easy task. Without arms I had no way to go through the crawling stage and no way to break my fall when my left foot tripped my right and sent me sprawling. After my first few painful attempts at walking on my own, I sat down in the middle of the living-room floor and refused to try again. Dad bribed me with sweets; he threatened me; he begged me to conspire with him to surprise Mom. But I just sat there, glaring up at him.

One afternoon just before my mother's arrival, Dad left me alone in the living room—or so I thought. Apparently he had deliberately draped my favorite stuffed bear over the edge of the kitchen table. When I spotted it there, I scooted on my back across the living-room rug. I could scoot face-up—shoulders squirming and legs pumping—as fast as any normal child could crawl. Maybe faster. Everyone worried that I would cut my back on a carpet nail or bang my head against a wall; but when I got up to speed, scooting along on my backside, nobody could catch me to stop me.

So I scooted to the table and lay there looking up at my bear's legs dangling just out of reach. For a moment I kicked at the table, trying to get the bear to fall. (It was a trick I had learned early in my armless life.) But the bear was stubborn and didn't move. I scooted back to that green-velvet Salvation Army sofa, maneuvered myself up against it by pushing my feet against the carpet, and then turned my face toward the sofa, shifting my legs into a kneeling position.

All that was left to do was stand. So I stood. Wiggling my chest back and forth and shifting my weight from leg to leg, I moved up the front of the sofa like an inchworm crawling up the trunk of a tree. I was limping toward the table, trying to keep my balance, when Dad came out cheering and applauding from his hiding place behind the kitchen door.

"You did it, you little devil," he said. "I left you alone and you did it! Look at you: you're walking."

Of course, at just that moment I lost my balance and fell against the iron legs of the kitchen table, splitting my chin and bleeding profusely. It was the first of a million split chins. What else can you do but fall on your face when you have no arms? God must have known how important my chin would be; I heal fast there. But if you look closely, you can count the scars on my chin like rings on a redwood tree.

Dad cleaned and bandaged the wound, then took me out to dinner. He loved Italian food. On those rare occasions when we ate out, Dad ordered a large helping of spaghetti and enough plates to share his meal with all the children. When Mom was with us, she would cut the spaghetti into perfect little pieces and spoon them neatly into my mouth. But Dad taught me how to eat alone.

"There, Tony," he said, sliding a plate onto the aluminum tray of the restaurant high chair. "It's all yours."

I looked at the plate of spaghetti covered in red sauce and waited for him to cut it into spoon-sized portions and shovel them into me. But Dad, eating from his own plate, was ignoring me completely. What does a little kid with no arms do at a time like that?

It didn't take long to figure it out. I just ducked my head down into my plate and began to slurp up the long, delicious pasta.

In the ensuing years I grew fairly graceful at the process. But I wish I had a video-tape of that first attempt at dining out with Dad. I can imagine the other people in that cheap little pizza place watching my father eating politely, as he had been reared—and his almost-three-year-old son dropping his face open-mouthed into the spaghetti and rising up with noodles dangling, mouth chewing, and forehead, nose, and lips dripping red with sauce.

•

THE SURPRISE

Mom, who had never flown before, was scheduled to fly into Los Angeles on Monday afternoon. Dad was waiting with me near her gate at the end of the long concourse. Mom remembers that she and the children—José in one arm and little Mayella in the other—were the last to leave the plane. Dad had grown restless, worrying that we had missed her. When they finally spotted each other, Dad rushed up to hug my mother, folding all of us in his embrace.

"I have a little surprise," he whispered after kissing Mom, José, and Mayella.

At that moment he set me down on the red carpet that ran the length of the airport waiting room. Mom remembers gasping as I tottered back and forth, looking up at her. She says I grinned as though I really had conspired with my father in his surprise. My brother hurried to hold me up.

"No, José," Dad said quietly. "Let Tony walk by himself."

As if on cue, I smiled at José, turned toward the center of the room, and limped off at the head of the parade. Mom cried. She says that Dad cried too, but that he tried to hide his tears. We were a strange parade that day. They say that everyone we passed in the airport stopped to watch the tiny little kid with no arms and a heavily bandaged chin limping through the crowded airport with his excited, happy family close behind.

6. The Urge to Fly

"Look, Tony," my mother exclaimed, "Auntie brought you new red shoes!"

Learning to walk was definitely a mistake, or so it seemed to me during those first few months of walking. As a reward for my achievement, everybody gave me shoes. Until that time I had never worn shoes. I needed my toes free to do what fingers do for other children. But people didn't understand that—not even my mom and dad. They all kept covering my toes with shoes. White and brown dress shoes, red, blue, and yellow tennis shoes, shoes in every shape and color piled up in our apartment as aunts and uncles, friends and neighbors all dropped in to cheer me as I charged about.

"Look at Tony," they would shout. "He's *walking*. Bravo! Good boy, Tony. Great work, little guy. Come to Uncle. See what Auntie brought you? A brand-new pair of shoes!"

It was awful. There seemed to be no way to escape the gift of shoes. Still, happy to be in the limelight, I let them put the shoes on my feet. Then, to please them further, I limped at full speed around our apartment in Inglewood, favoring my short left leg, lurching occasionally into a piece of furniture, slipping now and then on throw rugs, landing often on my face, and occasionally breaking open the much-scarred chin. Except for the falls, everybody loved my performance, and those cute little baby shoes just kept piling up.

Mom recalls that I would wear the shoes just long enough to please the relatives who gave them. Then, she says, when the family wasn't looking, I would sneak out of the room, lie on my back, and kick madly until the shoes flew off and I was barefoot and comfortable once again.

Those ten toes were more important to me than anyone could imagine. By my fourth or fifth birthday, I could use my toes almost as well as other children could use their fingers. I could pick up toys and even fling them across the room. I could build towers and bridges with my rubber building blocks; I could maneuver tiny cars across the floor in races with José. With my toes I could hold a hand of cards, tune the radio, grip a hammer, pound round wooden pegs into holes, and even pinch my brother's rear end when he teased me or tried to boss me around.

As a baby I used my toes to hold my rattle, my bottle, and my teething ring. And before I was two, Mom wedged a crayon between my toes, placed a blank piece of drawing paper on the floor in front of me, and encouraged me to sketch away. From that day on I drew hundreds of pictures. Mom and Dad, typical parents, pinned them up on the wall and taped them to the refrigerator door.

MY FIRST ARM

Mom recalls that whenever I drew the picture of a person, I gave that person arms. I didn't have arms, hands, or fingers myself, but I knew that they were important. As I began to use crayons and pencils to create worlds of my own, I refused to people them with deformed or handicapped children. And though I felt perfectly able to get along with just feet and toes myself, my dad and mom were working hard to place arms on me just as I placed arms on the people I drew.

In 1966 the March of Dimes brought together a team of specialists from the University of California and doctors from Orthopaedic Hospital in Los Angeles for a Child Amputee Prosthetics Project. There were hundreds of children in the Los Angeles area who had lost all or a portion of an arm or leg in an accident. Others, like me, had lost arms or legs through birth defects. Against my protests, Mom and Dad signed me up as a candidate for the Prosthetics Project. After several months of waiting, I was one of the children chosen to be fitted for an artificial arm. Everybody was excited about that opportunity except me. I hated the idea.

My feet and toes did almost everything an arm, a hand, or fingers could do, and a whole lot more than that plastic-and-metal contraption with a hook dangling where a hand should be. But Mom and Dad wanted me to have every possible help in overcoming my "handicap." At great personal price in time and energy, they took me to Orthopaedic Hospital for all of the artificial arm fittings and the training that followed.

The doctors decided that I should begin with one arm only. Technicians produced a harness that fit over my right shoulder and supported an upper arm made of a plastic shell, a metal elbow joint that locked and unlocked, a lower arm made of a second plastic shell, and a metal wrist joint to which they attached a shiny metal hook that opened and closed like a thumb and forefinger.

Needless to say, I hated that hook and the plastic-and-metal arm to which it was attached. Learning to use it was a nightmare. A thin steel cable hung down from the shoulder harness and was attached to my right leg. When I shrugged or stretched my shoulder correctly, the cable would tighten and my arm would move up and down. When I shrugged my shoulder and moved my right leg in just the right sequence, the hook would open and close enough to grasp an object and hold it in place.

My parents, the doctors at Orthopaedic Hospital, and the scientists at UCLA all meant well, but I didn't want to wear or use my artificial arm. From the beginning I put it on only under protest. My feet and toes were fine for almost every task, and with practice I was becoming more and more skilled at using them.

For example, when I was five, the March of Dimes sponsored a drawing contest among its amputee children. I beat all the competition with pictures that I had drawn with crayons gripped between my toes. Mom still has the front-page newspaper story describing that contest. Two samples of my drawings are included in the article. One is the portrait of a little boy with wings and arms. He appears to be flying. His eyes and mouth are open wide with excitement, and his hair stands on end in the breeze. Far below him is the earth, a distant round globe. Looking back, I wonder if the picture was a self-portrait of the little boy I wanted to be, with wings and arms and in flight above the world.

Soon after we returned from our first visit to Central America, the Melendez household gained another member. My younger sister, Marylou, was born January 27, 1965. When she was born, José was six years old, I was four, and my sister Mayella was just two and a half. For the next two years we lived in that two-bedroom apartment in Inglewood near the Los Angeles International Airport. We four children shared one bedroom—and it was wonderful.

As we grew older, there was never a boring moment. We turned that small bedroom into a playground. The beds became jungle gyms or trampolines. We used brooms and mops to prop our sheets and blankets into tents, and the four of us performed circus acts beneath the big top we thereby created. At other times we were animals in a zoo, prisoners in a jail, doctors and nurses doing surgery in a hospital, soldiers at war.

We pushed the beds together to form a stage on which we performed our original plays or musicals. We pushed the beds back against the walls to form a skating rink or bull-fight arena. We built imaginary cities with cardboard walls and penciled-in windows. We drew and painted. We formed figures from clay and papier-mâché. Mom and Dad had almost no money, but they provided us the raw materials and taught us how to improvise.

As we reached school age, José walked to a nearby elementary school, and later a bus took me to Inglewood Orthopedic School. There teachers taught me the regular elementary school subjects, while therapists trained me in basic survival skills and showed me how to use the awkward mechanical arm. Mayella and Marylou were too young for school; they stayed home with Mom—or with an aunt, if Mom was out selling Amway or any of the other products she sold to supplement Dad's small income.

During those five years between 1964 and 1969 when we lived in Inglewood, Dad worked any and every job he could find. On weekends he worked, studied English, and attended neighborhood citizenship classes, dreaming of that day when he would have his citizenship papers and the chance to be professionally certified in America through the special program promised him at Cal Poly.

Mom remembers how hard Dad studied for his test to qualify as a United States citizen. On the day he was to be tested, Mom packed a lunch, and Dad drove the family to San Bernardino, where the citizenship test was to be administered.

"I sat with you children on the lawn of the city hall in San Bernardino," Mom remembers. "After lunch your father kissed me and then hugged each of you for good luck. He marched across the lawn and up the slate steps as if going off to war. In his shirt pocket were three sharpened pencils with new erasers. In the back pocket of his pants was his well-worn paperback English dictionary. He turned and waved to us before entering the building, and we waved back."

"*Buena suerte, Papá,*" José cried. "Good luck, Daddy!"

We all knew what the test meant to him. As a citizen, he could enter the special certification program at the university. With his diploma as an agricultural specialist, he could get a good job with work he could be proud of, regular hours and days off, and medical benefits for himself and for his family. Without that certification, he might have to go on sweeping out sweat shops, mowing lawns, and facing daily humiliation for minimum wage.

At first we played games on the lawn as we waited for the test to end. Then, as the hour drew near, we gathered around Mom and watched the courthouse door with growing anxiety. Suddenly he appeared. Other immigrants were shaking Dad's hand, and he was smiling proudly. He waved at us and held up both arms in a gesture of triumph.

"*Gracias a Dios*!" Mom exclaimed.

"Daddy!" José cried, jumping to his feet and running to meet him.

Three days later he stood in a large auditorium with hundreds of other new Americans.

"I pledge allegiance," he said, his lips trembling and his knees knocking, "to the United States of America."

Soon, he thought, I will be standing before the dean at Cal Poly.

"And to the republic for which it stands . . ."

I will tell him that I am now an American. Now he can admit me to his program.

"One nation, under God, with liberty and justice for all."

Now I too will begin my pursuit of happiness, he thought.

The day after they handed Dad his proof of citizenship, he drove to the university, walked quickly across the campus, and boldly opened the door to the office of his academic counselor.

"Now I am a citizen," he said proudly. "Now I can be enrolled in your certification program."

The man must have been confused at first. Years had passed since my father had been turned away. During that time the state legislature had made serious cuts in the budget, and Dad's program had been canceled.

"Congratulations, Mr. Melendez," he said quietly, looking at the file his secretary had just placed in his hands, "but the program you want has been canceled."

For a moment the news didn't sink in.

"Canceled?" my father whispered. "How could that be?"

After trying to explain how state government works, how programs can be canceled or vetoed in midstream, the empathetic counselor took my dad's arm and led him to the door.

"Good luck, Mr. Melendez," he muttered, never dreaming that he and his canceled program were the beginning of the end of my father's life.

THE BEGINNING OF THE END

It isn't hard to piece together the process that led to my father's deterioration and eventually to his death. The first step was his move from Rivas to Los Angeles. He was like a fish out of water here. He longed for the soil, for the freshly plowed fields of home, for the young sugar-cane sprouts and the fresh running water that gave them life. Instead, he found himself waiting for piece-work on the shabby, smoggy, graffiti-ridden corners of east Los Angeles.

Still, he knew that only in America would he find the kind of medical treatment I needed, so he put his own dreams aside and began to dream for me. He was young, strong, and determined to provide for each of us—but especially, I believe, for me. Imagine his growing frustration as he tried to support us on the minimum-wage jobs that he could find. And there was no extra time or money to train in another field. Instead, he found himself in a huge pool of cheap labor as more and more unskilled young people migrated to America.

He worked at every job that he could find. He was a janitor, a night watchman, a gardener, a taxi driver, and a cashier in an all-night liquor store. In his extra moments he studied and practiced English, hoping that would lead him to a decent position. He underlined ads in the help-wanted sections of the daily Spanish-language paper and in the *Los Angeles Times*. He used the pay phone at the corner to call every number listed in the ads. But jobs were scarce, and the pay was impossibly low.

And almost every day it seemed that I had to be taken to another hospital or clinic for a test or for a fitting or for training for my artificial arm. The bus system was slow and terribly inconvenient. For a period of several months Uncle Tarcisio loaned Dad a car, and he often loaned it for an afternoon or a day. He was very generous. When I was seven, Dad had saved enough money to buy another used car of his own—his first since the Plymouth that had taken us back to Nicaragua. Unfortunately, that same used car, a Chevrolet, almost killed him.

THE ACCIDENT

Dad was working Saturdays as a gardener for the Los Angeles Rapid Transit District at the time. He pulled weeds and picked up trash along the highways. On Sundays he filled the old Chevy with gardening tools and drove it around the neighborhood, earning extra money cutting lawns and weeding flowerbeds. For a week or two the used car worked fine. Then one Monday afternoon it refused to start. Dad was stranded across town when the engine quit and refused to be revived.

My father opened the hood and began to work on the engine. He was alone, so he had to move back and forth between the engine and the front seat, trying to get the tired old car to come to life. He even got under the car, hoping to find the problem and to fix it.

After an hour of Dad's fiddling, the Chevy did start. He was exhausted by that time. As he crawled out from under the engine, the car began to roll forward. My father didn't see it coming; he had paused to rest on the street with his back to the moving Chevy. Just as he started to rise, the car ran into my father and knocked him back down to the pavement. Using his back and shoulders, he managed to stop the car's forward motion and keep it from running over him. But in the process, Dad nearly broke his back. By the time he had driven home, he was dizzy with the pain.

That same week Dad was hired to run a piece of heavy machinery in an auto-parts factory. For two days he tried to work in spite of the growing pain in his back, arms, and shoulders. Twice he fainted and collapsed on the job. On the third day, Dad was fired.

For a week my father lay in bed waiting for his back to heal. His doctor had warned him that he needed serious medical attention and several months in bed, but Dad had no money saved. He didn't want to risk a long stay in the hospital or the expense of surgery, so for that week he lay flat on his back, hoping that he would heal on his own. Dad's back didn't heal, although for months he struggled to recuperate. During those months he had no job—and therefore no income, no worker's compensation, and no unemployment benefits. It was hard on my father's pride, but for those months without work, Mom and Dad had to depend on their extended family to survive.

Mom's three aunts had good jobs in Los Angeles. For weeks they did all the shopping for my mother. One aunt would buy the meat we needed. The second aunt would buy cereal, rice, and beans. The third aunt would buy and deliver baby food and other supplies for Mayella and Marylou, who were still only infants at the time.

Mom's sister Muriel and her husband, René, also brought supplies, and Tarcisio stopped by with food and money to help us through. My mother even wrote to Grandpa and Grandma Rodriquez in Nicaragua, who sent a check to help us. Dad was too embarrassed to write his own parents in El Salvador. He wanted them to believe that he was succeeding in America. He couldn't stand the thought of being seen as the son who had failed and needed his parents to rescue him.

As my dad's back began to heal, he would take long walks around the neighborhood, trying to find a way out of his deepening despair. He tried to hide from Mother and the family his growing sense of failure and helplessness, but we knew he was troubled.

What Dad was experiencing, thousands of others just like him were feeling too. By 1969 immigrants, legal and illegal, were pouring into Los Angeles. Although some were taken in by relatives, others were on their own. Sometimes five or six families lived illegally in empty apartments in abandoned or condemned high-rise buildings. Like my father and mother, they had come to Los Angeles dreaming of new beginnings, hoping to build a better life for themselves and their families.

Unfortunately, for most of the immigrants, the dream was short-lived. There were few jobs, and food, clothes, and housing were expensive. They were living "lives of quiet desperation," in the words of the American writer Thoreau. Unemployed men lined up early in the morning for day-laborer jobs. Walls and sidewalks, buses and billboards were sprayed with angry, desperate graffiti. Armed robberies were commonplace throughout the city. People were unemployed, hungry, sick, and growing more and more afraid—and my father was there in the midst of them.

"He never talked about his pain," Mom told me. "He kept it bottled up inside. But I could sense it growing there. I began to feel helpless myself. I loved your dad; he was a good man. He loved me and he loved his children, but his own dreams were dying, and I didn't know what to do to help him."

LOS ANGELES INTERNATIONAL AIRPORT

Dad used to drive his Chevy to the Los Angeles International Airport, park in lot C, and ride the shuttle to the terminal. He spent hours walking up and down the long corridors. He would stare up at the boards announcing flight arrivals and departures, then sit on a bench overlooking the old customs area and watch people arriving from around the world.

My dad never told us why he spent so much time at the airport. It was an exciting place to visit, of course, and he could always find crowds of people there, even in the middle of the night. But why he spent so much time there is a mystery. I was just a little kid and didn't know about his airport vigils then, much less consider what drove him to take those long, lonely outings away from his family; but now, looking back, I think I know what he was thinking about as he walked through the nearly empty airport concourse in the middle of the night. And it makes me sad.

Dad was trapped in Los Angeles. There was no way for him to escape the cycle of poverty that he found himself in. Don't misunderstand: he loved the United States and was proud to have become a citizen; his citizenship certificate hung on the wall of our apartment next to his diploma from Rivas. But in Rivas he had had dreams for his life and for the life of his family. Now, in east Los Angeles, he saw those dreams collapse.

Still, my mother says that he never once complained about his fate. In fact, in the worst of times my father remained sensitive to other people's needs and was always ready to help them. At the airport, for example, Dad would see families arriving in the middle of the night from El Salvador or Nicaragua. He would introduce himself to them, talk about home, and answer their questions about the city.

"One night," my mother recalls, "your dad awakened me just before sunrise. I followed him into the living room of our second little apartment in Inglewood. A doctor from Nicaragua was standing there with his wife and two little children. They were emigrating to America. Their plane had been delayed, and in the confusion of their late arrival, their family had failed to meet them at the airport. Your father saw their predicament and invited them home for a rest and breakfast. They had no American money," she explained, "and the banks were closed. The hotels were full and very, very expensive. The people looked tired and confused, so he brought them home."

Such acts of charity were common for my father. Mom remembers getting up in the middle of many nights to find sheets and blankets to house strangers Dad had brought home. "They have no place to go," he would say. And Mom would get up gladly to cook a meal or prepare a place for the strangers to lie down and rest.

As soon as Dad's back had mended sufficiently (though not completely), he began to look for another job. After a six-month search, he was hired as a semiskilled worker by Parco, a large corporation that manufactured parts for airplanes. In an amazingly short time, Dad became skilled at molding gaskets and seals for aircraft engines. For the first time in Los Angeles, he was actually making slightly more than the minimum wage.

About that time—I was five or six—I broke into showbiz. Pictures of me drawing with a crayon held between my toes had been filed in the archives of the "Billy Barty Show" at the time I won the March of Dimes drawing contest. Apparently a producer scouting the archives for ideas spotted me one day and showed the newspaper story to America's most famous little person, Billy Barty himself. The next thing I new, Mom had me dressed in a white shirt with sleeves cut off and sewn together, matching white pants, and a bright-blue bowtie.

"These are the winning pictures," Billy Barty announced to the world as the television camera zoomed in on a closeup of my drawings of tugboats and brightly colored flowers.

"And this is the winning artist," he said, walking up to the platform on which I was seated.

"Well, how does it feel, Tony, to be on network television?"

Mom remembers that I sat staring at him, silent as a stone.

"You draw very well," the famous Billy Barty said, trying to get me into conversation. "Is it hard to draw with your toes?"

Mom says that I didn't even nod. I just sat there, staring at the wall and looking as if I was about to cry.

"That's okay, son," Mr. Barty whispered, bending close to me. "You'll talk when you're ready. Why don't you draw for us instead."

The paper and crayons lay on the stage in front of me. I grasped a blue crayon between my toes and began to sketch the sky. Then I picked up a brown crayon and began to draw a little boy with eyes and mouth wide open and hair blowing in the breeze. The little boy looked a lot like me, except that he had arms and wings and he was flying high above the earth.

I think I understand better now why my father hugged me and began to cry when he saw the picture that I had drawn. He too was earthbound; he too must have longed for wings to fly.

7. The Move to Chino

A notice written in English and Spanish and headlined "Important News for Parco Employees" was posted on the bulletin board near my father's workstation. At the noon break, Dad paused with other workers to read the four short paragraphs that would make him tremble. Company management had voted to move Parco's molding plant to Chino, a suburb almost fifty miles east of Los Angeles. Just when my father felt his luck had changed, bad news struck again.

"We either move to Chino," Dad told my mother later that day, "or I have to find another job."

"Where's Chino?" Mom asked.

My father didn't know. So on Sunday the family climbed into Uncle René's car and drove due east across Los Angeles County to the tiny town that soon would become our home.

"We drove out the San Bernardino Freeway," my mom remembers. "For forty miles there was nothing but office buildings, shopping malls, high-rise apartments, gas stations, and parking lots as far as you could see. Then we turned off the freeway at Euclid Avenue and drove south toward Chino."

"Suddenly everything changed," she told me. "On both sides of the road, green fields stretched out as far as you could see. There were dairy cows grazing around tiny lakes. Wildflowers bloomed everywhere. We spotted five or six teenagers riding horseback across the road ahead, and a stable where horses could be rented. The sky was deep blue, and in the distance you could see fleecy white clouds hugging the foothills and snow-capped Mount Baldy."

My father was ecstatic. He had begun that day with dread in his heart. One of our neighbors in Inglewood had warned him that Chino was "a nothing little town" where the state of California had prisons for men, women, and even children. But the gently rolling countryside, cultivated fields, and flat pastures around Chino reminded Dad of Rivas and of home.

"We're going to move," my father whispered. "We're going to move to Chino!"

During those next few weeks, my father read everything he could find about Chino. He learned that there were just 10,305 people living in the sixteen square miles that made up the little town. And 1,700 acres of that same land had been designated by the city planners as "an agricultural preserve."

On our long drive from Los Angeles that day, my father had seen the county's countless hillsides scarred and bulldozed to make way for endless tracts of houses. But Chino's city leaders had decided to guarantee that houses wouldn't cover their fertile and productive land. We saw fields of tomatoes, corn, strawberries, melons, onions, and seedflowers growing in profusion. And Chino's family-owned dairy herds included over 250,000 cows and produced more than one million gallons of milk every day.

Just 200 years earlier, Indians had roamed this golden valley between San Bernardino and Pasadena. In the early 1800s a young Spaniard named Don Antonio María Lugo began to build a 47,000-acre ranch that would stretch from the San Bernardino Mountains to the present-day port city of San Pedro. He named his holdings Rancho Santa del Chino, after his patronness, Saint Anne of the Fair Hair.

My father loved the coincidence. From childhood he had carried the nickname Chelle—Spanish slang for a male with light-blond hair. And Chino was the nickname for Saint Anne, whose hair and skin were fair like my father's.

THE HOUSE ON ESSEX STREET

Within a few weeks Dad found a rental listing in the *Los Angeles Times* for a little two-bedroom house on Essex Street in Chino. Once again we all piled into Uncle René's station wagon for the journey across Los Angeles County. After entering Chino, we drove down Ramona Avenue, turned right on Phillips Street, and then made an immediate left onto tiny Essex Street.

"Not a through street," a sign warned us.

"Good," said my father. "We're not passing through anyway. We're going to live right here."

Dad was right. We moved to Essex Street in 1966 and we've lived in the same house on that same street ever since. Our neighbors are Japanese-American farmers whose fields begin directly across our dusty asphalt street, and just fifty feet north of our little brown-and-tan tract house stands a large aluminum-sided shed where our neighbors store their farm equipment, their seed and fertilizer, and their boxes of ripe red tomatoes and dark-green chives on the way to market.

Tarcisio borrowed a large pickup truck and moved us to Chino five days later. The little house we rented in 1966 (and purchased for $12,000 in 1970) was a typical California tract house. Made of wood and stucco with dark-brown walls, tan trim, and a gray-green asphalt-shingled roof, it had about 1,300 square feet of space. As we entered through the torn screendoor, we found to the left a combined dining room–kitchen area (furnished with a table just large enough to hold our family); to the right was the living room, with a picture window looking out across the fields of chives and tomatoes. Down a short hallway there were two bedrooms, one bathroom, and a small one-car garage. The tire-tracked front lawn had been used as a parking space, and the equally scruffy rear yard was dusty and unplanted.

Mom and Dad took the small bedroom nearest the kitchen, while José, Mayella, Marylou, and I shared the second bedroom, just three long steps down the hallway. Dad built a set of bunkbeds for us boys and two twin beds for the girls. José was nine years old when we moved into the house on Essex Street. I was seven, Mayella was six, and Marylou was four.

We loved our bedroom immediately. It was our own private space, and we filled it with excitement. One day soon after moving we transformed the room into Metropolis, home of Clark Kent and Lois Lane. I sat on top of the bunkbeds watching my big brother swoop about the room in Superman's bright-red cape (Mom's bedspread). Suddenly I was inspired to join Superman in the skies above Metropolis.

"No," José yelled, as I stood on my tiptoes on the top bunkbed, high above my open-mouthed brother and my two startled sisters.

"Superman!" I yelled, launching myself head-first into the space between us.

At that moment, alarmed by José's excited cry, Mom ran into the room. She got there just in time to see me hit the hard wooden edge of Mayella's twin bed with my already weathered chin. There was nothing else to break my fall.

Mom recalls the pandemonium that followed. I was screaming and bleeding profusely. The girls were crying and rushing about the room. José got a towel from the bathroom and helped Mom to stop the bleeding and then stayed with the girls while Mom took me to the emergency room. It took nine stitches to sew up the wound. Our new room had been baptized in blood.

CYPRESS ORTHOPEDIC SCHOOL

Gradually I learned to take better care of myself, thanks in no small part to Cypress Orthopedic School in nearby Ontario, where Mom enrolled me shortly after we moved to Chino. The long red-brick building on the corner of Park Place and Tenth Street was surrounded by green lawns and white poplar trees. There were four regular classrooms on the south side of the school. The larger therapy rooms and school offices were just across a wide tiled hall that cut the building in half. From the classroom windows we could see several acres of playground: an asphalted area with game squares painted on the surface, a colorful jungle gym, and grassy fields prepared for baseball, kickball, and soccer.

Cypress Orthopedic School enrolled physically and emotionally handicapped students from first through the eighth grades. Every morning a yellow van specially equipped for wheelchairs pulled up outside my door on Essex Street and transported me to the Cypress campus. Sometimes the van took two full hours to cover the short distance, because each student required special help in getting on or off. I could have walked the distance faster.

The classrooms weren't unlike normal elementary school classrooms. Each came equipped with colorful bulletin and chalk boards, bookshelves and display areas, and a teacher's desk with an American flag standing nearby. But we didn't have desks. We had individual tables just tall enough for a wheelchair to fit beneath.

In the classrooms we studied all the usual elementary school subjects: reading, writing, and arithmetic. But the lessons progressed slowly, because most of the students needed special help for their physical handicaps or learning disabilities. Each classroom had one trained attendant for every ten children, to help classmates who couldn't eat or drink, dress or use the toilet, write or even turn pages by themselves. All of my classmates were handicapped, but the teachers and therapists at Cypress preferred to call us "handi-capable."

We also had therapy sessions scheduled throughout the day, where we learned the arts of survival. On my second day at Cypress my therapist took one look at the scars on my chin and decided that she would teach me how to fall without bruising or cutting myself. Most children have arms, hands, and elbows to break a fall. I had only my chin, and it was pretty well battered by my sixth birthday.

"Stand on the blue mat, Tony," my therapy technician ordered. "Now let me show you how to fall so that your chin won't get split open again."

Suddenly the therapist herself began to fall with a loud groan—a tall woman falling right on her face before me. I had never seen a teacher fall over in a classroom, and it struck me as funny. First falling like a great cut tree, she then bent forward into a ball, rolled onto her right shoulder, did a complete somersault, and rose to her feet again as gently as a kitten.

"Now you try it," she said, smiling back at me.

I hesitated.

"*Try* it," she urged quietly. "The mat is soft, and I'll help you."

The next thing I knew, I felt her strong, firm hands around me, and I was rolling into a ball and somersaulting down the mat as lightly as a feather.

"Well done!" she said as I started to leave the mat, proud of my achievement.

"Now do it again," she said. I frowned at her. One fall seemed plenty. I had mastered her trick. Why should I do it again?

"Do it again!" she said, in spite of my frown. "Only this time," she added, "do it without my help."

I decided to appease her. She seemed nice enough. Maybe after a second roll she would leave me alone. I flopped to the mat, rolled into a ball, and almost broke my neck.

"Good job," she said. I was still seeing stars when she added, "Now do it again—only this time don't land on your head. Tuck your shoulder in and roll."

I suppose that in the next seven years at Cypress I heard Mrs. Cheavers say, "Good, Tony—now do it again!" at least a zillion times.

I didn't care much one way or the other about any of those exercises, but there was one backbreaker that we did on a long, round canvas pillow shaped like a Tootsie Roll that I hated with a vengeance. Starting the first day, Mrs. Cheavers had me lying face-down on that hard round mat with my head and shoulders hanging over one end and my feet hanging down across the other.

"Okay, Tony," she would say, "lift your chest and head high and hold them there!"

I would obey. Briefly.

"No, Tony," she would urge quietly, "keep your head and chest up until I tell you to relax."

I would strain to lift my head and chest up above the mat, balancing in the air like a diver soaring above the cliffs of Acapulco. Over and over again she would make me do it.

"Keep it up there, Tony," she would say, and I would groan and moan in protest.

"Because you have no arms, you have to grow strong in your neck and chest," she explained. "You're going to be using those muscles all the rest of your life. Make them tough," she would say.

And I would strain to obey her. Until she walked away to help another student, of course. Then I'd duck and run.

Actually, I didn't run too well at the beginning. My clubfoot and short leg still caused discomfort, but I tried for Mrs. Cheavers. I favored my left leg with a kind of rollicking sailor's limp. Mrs. Cheavers also had me walking on a board six inches above the mat, jumping rope, and even climbing up and down a short wooden ladder.

MY SECOND MECHANICAL ARM

I didn't know it at first, but the therapists were preparing me for a new mechanical arm. I tried to explain to them that I had already tried a false arm and had hated and finally rejected it. No matter what I did to prove to them that I could get by with just my two feet and ten little toes, they insisted that I learn to use the artificial limb that had been fit for me.

I hated that plastic-and-metal monster.

"But Tony, you'll need it to be independent," they would say. "Remember all the things you can't do without arms."

I knew exactly what they were referring to. There was an embarrassing moment in my short past—one that I would have liked to forget. Apparently my mother had passed it on to them. I was five at the time, and we lived in Inglewood; I had just started to attend Inglewood Orthopedic School. And I was afraid of just one thing: having to go to the bathroom at the wrong time and in the wrong place.

It didn't happen often. I had learned when to drink my milk or juice and when not to drink it. And I knew exactly when someone whom I trusted would be around to help me in the bathroom when I needed it. In that nightmare experience from my past, I got off schedule. In the middle of a kindergarten class I got the urge to urinate—and it was urgent. My teacher was new, a young woman unknown to me. My classmates were all strangers; there wasn't one I trusted. José was at his own school out there somewhere in Inglewood and my dad was at work, but I knew that Mom was at home.

We had had a telephone installed in our apartment, and I reasoned that if I made a big enough scene, someone just might call my mother. So I sat down in the middle of the kindergarten classroom, crossed my legs tightly, and began to howl.

The teacher tried to console me. She repeatedly asked me what was wrong, but I wouldn't reply. A supervisor was called, and of course I wouldn't tell her either. Telling would be humiliating, even for a kindergartner. So I just poured on the steam as my miserable howls echoed up and down the hallways.

Finally, in desperation, they called Mom.

"Mrs. Melendez, something is wrong with your son. He's terribly upset, and we don't know why. You'd better come to the school."

Mom couldn't drive, so she called my father at Parco. "Chelle," she said frantically, "something's wrong with Tony. Please come home now and take me to his school."

Dad ran to the office of his supervisor, explained the emergency, and broke every speed and safety law getting Mom and himself to the school. Believe it or not, while all of this was happening, I was still holding it. I had waited for almost an hour—an amazing feat. I should have been rewarded, to my mind; but when the principal came running into the room, followed by the school nurse, my mother, my father, and the anguished teacher, I had a suspicion that they might respond in quite another way. Still I howled.

"What's the matter, Tony?" my mother asked.

"I've got to go to the bathroom," I whispered into her ear.

For about ten seconds my mother looked at me in shock. Then she began to laugh. The next thing I knew, she was whispering the news to Dad, and Dad whispered it to the teacher, and the teacher whispered it to the principal. As my mother hustled me from the room, I could hear them begin laughing, one by one, as the news spread.

CAPTAIN HOOK

So the therapists at Cypress had decided that the only way I could really be independent was by learning to use a mechanical arm. Even as a small child I had thought my toes and feet would be enough, but they were convinced that I needed that plastic-and-metal contraption to eat, dress, use the toilet, and generally keep myself clean and tidy. I preferred to get by with a little help from my friends.

I lost. Once again I was fitted for an artificial arm that attached to my shoulder. A tan plastic upper arm and a tan plastic forearm were separated by a mechanically locking elbow joint. On the harness just below my chin were two buttons that locked and unlocked the elbow. By shrugging my shoulders in just the right way, I could move the arm up and down or swing it to the right or left. A wire cable extended from my shoulder harness down to my right leg to allow me to operate the metallic hook with my leg.

I was six years old. Not surprisingly, when they draped the harness around my shoulder, attached the cable to my leg, and dangled the arm in place, I felt trapped and uncomfortable. But I tried. Wearing the arm made me feel hot and sticky, and it weighed a ton. Needless to say, I couldn't wait to get it off after practice.

Worse than everything else, I felt embarrassed wearing the arm. My friends didn't make it any easier. They loved to catch me on the playground or in my front yard and pull the arm out like a wing. It was hard to retract it by myself, so I had to walk around with the artificial arm sticking straight out like a broken wing until a parent or teacher intervened or I could force the arm closed against a wall or doorway.

Sometimes in class I would raise the hook when other children were raising their hands. But many times when their hands came down, my hook stayed up in the air and I had to have a teacher push it into place again. Other times, running across the playground, I would snag the arm on a wall or tree as I passed and end up with the arm sticking straight out behind me.

On top of the inconvenience and embarrassment, my friends all called me Captain Hook. My mother wondered why I insisted on carrying the arm back home from school in a special canvas bag she had made for me, and my teachers wondered why the arm was constantly being retrieved by a custodian or grounds' monitor from deep in the bushes or from behind a tree. I lost or hid that arm on every possible occasion. Still, for six long elementary school years, the therapists made me wear it.

I knew in my heart that for the rest of my life, my feet would be my hands and my toes would be my fingers. I determined that I would learn to do everything that a normal ten-fingered child could do with my ten pudgy little toes. Early on I amazed everybody with what I could accomplish. Eventually even my therapists began to take notice.

WHO NEEDS ARMS?

"I remember the first time you beat me at jacks," my sister Mayella told me recently. "You were about ten, and you sat down beside me on the linoleum floor in the kitchen. You tossed the ball with one foot, snagged up a jack with the other, and caught the ball again. I couldn't believe it."

Actually, I could pick up as many as ten jacks with one foot. I could write class essays and do math problems with a thick pencil stuck between my toes. And I could eat—without making messes—by just bending down over my plate and using my lips and teeth to pick up food and then brushing my face against a napkin lying on the table.

I learned to dress myself by tossing a loose shirt onto my bed with my foot, buttoning the buttons with my toes, tossing the shirt in the air, and ducking under it as it parachuted down. Once I got the hang of it, it was easy to squirm into pants, and with sandals there was never a need to lace or tie my shoes.

And my toes got stronger and more accurate as I practiced. I could pick up a key to the house with my toes and unlock the door without a problem. My mom taught me to crochet (but I quit when a grinning neighbor boy asked me to crochet a shawl for his mother). With my big toe I could dial the telephone, turn on the television, start the water in our shower or tub, turn pages of my textbooks, and pack my knapsack for school.

I could wedge a toothbrush between the mirror and the sink and rub my teeth back and forth on it, or wedge a long-handled brush there to brush my hair. I could place soap or shampoo on a ledge and work up quite a lather. And I learned to use the toilet without calling for help.

I could grip almost anything between my chin and the top of my shoulder, including a crossbow and arrow, a hockey stick, a telephone receiver, and a rake or hoe. And I beat every kid at Cypress playing pool with the cue stick wedged between my shoulder and my chin.

One afternoon, when a taffy pull was scheduled for the students at Cypress, the teachers discussed how to include the little boy with no arms. Even they had to admit that my mechanical arm would only make a mess of things.

"Why don't we let him use his feet?" Mrs. Cheavers suggested to the other therapists (in a kind of victory for me over the mechanical arm).

"His *feet*?" another therapist cut in. "In our fresh homemade taffy?"

"Why not?" Mrs. Cheavers responded. "We can scrub his feet with a brush—and even disinfect them if you insist."

I did spend a lot of time barefoot, so my feet were stained and callused; but the teachers finally decided to give it a try. They scrubbed my feet and set me down with the other children around a huge metal bowl of warm, sticky taffy.

"Okay, kids," Mrs. Cheavers directed, "before we dip into the taffy, we need to butter our fingers . . . or our toes," she added. The next thing I knew, she was smearing butter all over my feet and toes. The other kids took small lumps of the gooey stuff in their fingers and watched as my feet plunged into the bowl and deftly picked up a larger lump of taffy for myself.

Before long we were all laughing and pulling taffy—stretching that wonderful sticky stuff and eating all the extra strands that we could. My toes did their job perfectly. I even managed to wrap a few pieces to take home to my brother and sisters.

"You made this with your *toes*?" Mayella asked, groaning and throwing her piece into the trash.

"It's good," Marylou chimed in, "*really* good." So poor Mayella had to fish her piece from the can and try it for herself.

Teachers, parents, brother, and sisters were all pleased with my new taffy-pulling skills. But the next day the poor custodian at Cypress voiced his complaint angrily. "Who made those butter-and-taffy footprints up and down the hallway?" he asked. "It took me half the night to scrape them all away."

8. A Trip to Rivas

With two full-time jobs and extra work on weekends, my father didn't have much spare time for watching television. But there were two programs he tried to see every week. We were a Lawrence Welk family, and the six of us never missed his program during those childhood years in Chino. And almost every Sunday evening, promptly at six, my father would stop whatever he was doing and herd the whole family toward our battered old television set in the living room. It was time for "Wild Kingdom," a thirty-minute series featuring a gray-haired older gentleman named Marlin Perkins and his adventures with wild animals around the world.

My father sat on the sofa surrounded by the four of us children, while Mom made Sunday-evening supper in the kitchen. When Marlin Perkins announced the animal of the week, my father would lean forward, reach into the clutter on top of the coffee table at his feet, and pull out an old green-and-yellow book. *The Mammals,* one of my dad's prized possessions, was a textbook he had first studied at the International Academy of Agriculture in Rivas.

The Spanish-language edition of the book was divided into sections. First each order of mammal was described (for example, "Order: *Rodentia*—squirrels, gophers, mice, porcupines, and beavers"). Then there were pictures of individual families within the order (for example, "Family: *Sciuridae*—squirrels"). Then came a detailed description of the characteristics of each genus within that family (for example, "Genus: *Spermophilus*—ground squirrels").

Marlin Perkins would be talking about ground squirrels from the television screen, but my father would be far ahead of him, describing in detail the white-tailed antelope squirrel of Mexico or the Rio Grande ground squirrel, common to all of Central America.

"You can always tell a Rio Grande squirrel," my father might say, reading from his book during the commercial, "by the cinnamon-colored patch on his nose and the pure white ring around his eyes. You'll see!" my father would add. "On our next trip to Rivas we'll spot a Rio Grande squirrel along the highway."

"Our next trip to Rivas" was perhaps my father's favorite expression. He loved America, but he longed for home. Mom wasn't sure if those television travelogues relieved my father's homesickness or simply made it worse. He spoke to my mother often of his plan to live six months of each year in the United States and six months in Central America, but there was never enough money to pay our monthly bills, let alone to set up housekeeping in two different worlds 5,000 miles apart.

But every four years my father somehow managed to save just enough money to make the trip home, with the help of Mother's extra income. She still sold Amway products to her Spanish-speaking friends and neighbors, and she bought radios, stereos, and beauty products and health aids to sell in Central America, as she had on that first trip.

The journey to visit my dad's folks in El Salvador and my mom's family in Rivas was long and exhausting. Sometimes, when Dad was especially homesick or in a hurry, we drove around the clock. That wasn't an ideal way for four young children to travel, but we didn't have money for motels. We slept in the car as my father drove, or we stopped along the highway when he just couldn't stay awake any longer. We didn't have money for restaurant meals either, so we packed a huge seven- to ten-day lunch and bought other food supplies from markets along the way. We bathed in streams or swam in the sea to clean our hot, sticky bodies, and we used bushes or clumps of trees for our toilet.

It wasn't easy for six of us, along with our baggage and the "contraband" my mother took to pay the bills, to fit inside the tired old station wagons that my father bought to make the journeys. We were crowded together for 4,531 miles in each direction. Our lungs were caked with dust, our lips were chapped, our bottoms were sore, and our muscles were stiff; but looking back, I don't remember anybody complaining much—even on the days our car broke down or ran out of gas and we were stranded high in the mountains in the early-morning cold or in the hot desert under a midday sun.

Despite the discomfort and inconveniences, we loved those family excursions. Every four years, for eight to ten wonderful weeks, we were together. And it was my father's energy and creativity that transformed those tedious journeys into unforgettable adventures.

DRIVING SOUTH

In 1972 Dad decided that the two-week school holiday at Christmas could be stretched four or five extra weeks to make our second family journey into Central America. José was twelve, I was ten, Mayella was nine, and Marylou was six when Dad loaded us into a 1965 blue Ford station wagon and headed south just three weeks before Christmas.

Something magical happened to my father when we hit the road together as a family. He literally became a different man. The oppression he felt in Los Angeles slipped farther away with each passing mile. He had the family singing before we reached San Diego, and by the time we crossed over into Mexico and began the drive down Highway 15 along the Sea of Cortez through Guaymas and Mazatlán toward Guadalajara and Mexico City, he was pointing out every important place along the way and regaling us with stories, myths, and legends.

Dad knew the names of practically every plant and animal we passed along the way. He could spot mineral deposits in the cliffs and rare orchids blooming along the highway. He knew legends about the native Indian tribes we passed and true stories about the Spanish conquistadors, missionary priests, outlaws, and saints who had lived and died along the roads we traveled.

In the little village of Los Mochis in the northwestern state of Sinaloa, we visited Mexico's largest sugar refinery. My father got out of the station wagon at the Miguel Hidalgo Dam and studied the irrigation system developed to water the cane fields. He may have been a menial laborer in Los Angeles, but on the road he was a professional keeping up with the changes in his chosen profession. He was preparing to spend long evenings with his friends from the refinery in Rivas, talking about planting, harvesting, and refining the cane.

In Guadalajara we bought fresh fruits and vegetables in Mexico's largest and most colorful open market. With his four children in tow, Dad walked up and down those rows of open stalls, describing each exotic fruit, sniffing the air with delight, and urging us to sample guava and melon slices, as well as fried bananas dipped in shredded coconut, and treating us all to fresh cups of mango and pineapple juice. In just minutes Dad could find and name forty different kinds of peppers on sale in that incredible market.

On the outskirts of Mexico City, Dad especially loved the pre-Columbian Aztec ruins in Teotihuacan. It felt as if Dad had driven that old blue Ford into a time machine as we entered the world of the Aztecs.

"Montezuma and his priests worshiped here," he would tell us, visibly moved by the huge pyramids: one erected to honor the sun, the other to honor the moon.

"The ancient Aztecs believed that the moon and the sun were born here," he would explain. He loved the Aztec legend of the two ancient gods who had the courage to throw themselves into a fire so that the day would be warmed and lighted by the sun and the long dark night would be cheered by the moon.

As we climbed the pyramids, huffing and puffing behind Dad, he would compare these monuments to the monuments of Egypt. "The base of the Pyramid of the Sun," he might say, "is just as big as the base of the great pyramid to Cheops in Egypt. Those Egyptian builders were good," he conceded, "but they can't beat the Aztecs of Mexico, no matter what people say."

We would scamper after Dad down the Street of the Dead, past the huge Citadel, to the Pyramid of Quetzalcoatl with its impressive stone carvings. He described each sculptured column and bas-relief along the way.

"No other civilization in the history of the world produced finer art than this," he said proudly. "This is *our* heritage too, and nothing in the Orient, India—even Greece or Rome—is more impressive than what the Aztec artists did right here where we're standing."

Leaving Mexico City, we could feel Dad's excitement mount as everything began to change around us. The eight-lane highways ended and the dusty dirt roads began as we navigated our way through southern Mexico. Dad steered us down the hairpin highway through jungles and swamps, up past rich green valleys, and high over forest-mantled peaks. He pointed out the volcanic summits of Popocatepetl, La Malinche, Toluca, and Colima—great mountains whose richly forested slopes hid fascinating Indian villages and thousands of years of almost forgotten history and culture.

After crossing the Mexican border into Guatemala, it wasn't long until we arrived at Lake Atitlán. "Half a century ago," Dad informed us, "the novelist Aldous Huxley called this the most beautiful lake in the world."

We climbed down a rocky pathway to the edge of the water as my father told his fascinating stories of this place.

"At exactly noon every day," he began, "each fishing boat or ferry, each canoe or sailboat from every village on the lake hurries into harbor. No one dares to be out on the lake when the *xocomil* might strike."

"*Xocomil*?" we all chorused together, stepping back from the waters of the lake. "What's a *xocomil*?"

"A strange wind," he answered mysteriously. "About noon it often sweeps across the lake, swamping boats and drowning everybody in them. And though scientists and professors from around the world have studied the lake, nobody knows for certain what causes the *xocomil*." Dad paused and smiled to himself. Then he added, "But I have my ideas . . ."

Then Dad would take our picture in front of the lake and we would all climb back into the station wagon, eager to ask our questions and even more eager to hear his wonderful replies about Lake Atitlán and her mysterious, deadly *xocomil*.

As we drove around the shores of that deep, blue lake, we could see in the distance the perfect cones of the four huge volcanoes whose eruptions dammed up the rivers that once flowed to the Pacific Ocean. Dad had endless tales to tell of the villages around Lake Atitlán.

"Each is different from the other," he explained as we drove from village to village, exploring ancient streets and colorful market-places. "Most of the villages were named after Christ's apostles," he said. "All the others were named after saints. But beyond that, the villages have little in common."

As Dad guided us around the lake, we could see for ourselves that the homes in Santiago were made from lava rock, cactus, and bamboo, while just a few miles away the houses of San Antonio were made of adobe and tile. In Tzununá the people lived in homes of mud and bamboo, while in nearby San Pedro, the homes were built from cement blocks with thick walls and colorful tile roofs.

Dad pointed out that each village specialized in a different handicraft. The people of San Pedro, for example, made ropes and hammocks from the fibers of the maguey plant; San Antonio artisans specialized in mats of reeds gathered from the lake; while Santiago was known for colorful cloth used in making blouses, sashes, and headdresses that flashed with orange, green, purple, and pink.

"Each village even grows its own special crop," Dad told us. He showed us coffee bushes being harvested in San Juan, oranges and lemons growing in the citrus groves of Tzununá, freshly planted onion fields in San Antonio, and avocado trees laden with fruit in San Pedro.

We were baffled and entertained. But as we drove toward Guatemala City, Dad peppered us with even more questions about the strange and wonderful villages of Lake Atitlán.

"Why do you think the people of San Pedro have lighter skin, hair, and eyes than all the rest?" he asked. "Why have the people of San Pedro become fervent evangelical Protestants," he queried, "while some nearby villages practice the traditional Catholic faith and still others cling to an ancient mixture of Christian and Mayan beliefs?"

We listened as Dad rehearsed questions that have been stumping the experts for centuries. "Why is the Santiago market run entirely by women?" he wondered. "And why do only the men of San Pedro use mules and horses to carry their loads?"

Dad loved the myths and traditions of Central America. Every new village along the way had something wonderful for my father to explain to us. I'll never forget one special Guatemalan village we visited. We had been bumping along a tortuous path high in the mountains. Recent rains had ruined the road. We were thirsty, tired, and hoping to find a place to stop and rest when we drove into the middle of a town that must have stopped its clocks 500 years ago.

A rough handpainted sign on a whitewashed wall read simply, "*Bienvenido* [Welcome]—Santa Catarina Palopó." The village of thatch-roofed houses had been built up the steep sides of a lush green hillside that seemed to plunge into Lake Atitlán. Old sandbags were still in place from floods that must have rushed regularly down the mountainsides through the dirt streets of the village.

As we entered Santa Catarina Palopó, there were signs of life—clothes drying on lines and bushes, dogs and cats lounging about, green and red peppers drying in the sun—but the streets were empty. There were no children playing beside the road. No old women stared at us from open doorways. No young men were at work in the fields at the edge of town. We thought at first that the town had been abandoned, but we were wrong.

Santa Catarina Palopó was having a fiesta to honor her patron saint. The entire village was gathered in or near the marketplace, selling and buying food and handicrafts, strolling in the park or plaza, or chatting on the steps of the cathedral as they waited for the midday mass of celebration to begin.

Dad had grown tired and grouchy from the long journey, but there was nothing like a celebration to bring him back to life again. He parked the car and led us into the middle of the festivities. He bought us each a plate of barbecued beef dripping with a wonderful sweet-hot salsa unique to Santa Catarina Palopó. There were crunchy onions fried in butter and fresh-roasted ears of corn on sticks. We sat on the curb and feasted while musicians played trumpets and guitars and dancers in long red, yellow, and green dresses whirled with their partners on the plaza square.

After our lunch Dad led us to the marketplace. Colorful handmade blankets, shawls, and serapes hung from rough wooden frames. Giant papier-mâché parrots stared down at us from their wire perches. Indian women knelt before primitive looms, weaving brightly colored yarns into beautiful blouses, skirts, headdresses, and sashes. We walked by a wall covered with life-sized papier-mâché masks. Dad explained that it wasn't Halloween, but that each angry or smiling face on the wall had a special meaning to the Indian artist who had created it, and a special task in the home or field where it would hang.

We followed the crowd as it moved back toward the cathedral. It wasn't unusual that the people were buying and carrying candles, but these candles were red, blue, green, and even black. As we neared the church, we noticed those variously colored candles burning on the front steps; inside, they graced little porticoes lining the walls and lit up the entire front altar. The building was ablaze with brightly colored candles.

After the mass, as we drove away from Santa Catarina Palopó, Dad explained that each candle represented a different kind of prayer request. People praying for a sick child left a blue candle for a boy or a pink candle for a girl. Farmers hoping for a good harvest left a green candle burning. An alcoholic struggling against his disease might leave a white candle, while husbands and wives seeking healing in their marriage might light a yellow candle for peace.

I had seen Dad buy a bright-red candle from a vendor. While we watched, he had lit it and knelt to pray. I still wonder why he chose a red candle, and what he was praying for that day.

GRANDPA AND GRANDMA MELENDEZ

El Salvador was the next stop on our journey. Dad was born in this, the smallest and most densely populated nation in Central America. In fact, with 4.2 million people (more than 500 per square mile), El Salvador is one of the most densely populated countries in the world. And though the people are poor and forced to scratch a living from the soil or the sea, the country is proud, lively, and beautiful beyond description.

Dad explained that El Salvador's first people, the Pipil Indian civilization, called El Salvador *Cuscutlan*, "the land of precious things." My father's homeland may be only 170 miles long and 60 miles wide, but her 8,000 square miles are rich in natural treasures. Twenty-two snow-capped volcanoes reign over moonscapes of shiny black lava, azure-blue volcanic lakes, rich ash-fertilized fields of coffee and cotton, coconut and citrus orchards, pine forests, and 230 miles of palm-shaded beaches.

Grandpa and Grandma Melendez's home in San Salvador, the nation's capital, was always our first real rest-stop on the journey south. Dad believed in staying equal amounts of time with both sets of grandparents. And though we grandchildren loved the Melendez and the Rodriquez families equally, the Melendez family was far more formal than our grandparents in Rivas.

The Melendez home occupied almost a full square block in the heart of the nation's capital, a beautiful, sprawling city of more than one million people. San Salvador was built in the shape of a cross; thus all four of the main boulevards intersecting the city ran together near the Plaza Barrios. Just south of the plaza Dad drove us past the National Palace, where the government was housed. The streets were choked with colorful little trucks and vintage taxis. The massive Metropolitan Cathedral dominated the plaza and the city.

San Salvador was built at the foot of the San Salvador volcano, and from its founding in 1545 the city has been shaken by countless major quakes and minor tremors. The fertile, mountain-ringed valley where San Salvador lies has been rocked up and down and back and forth so many times by earthquakes that the Indians called it the Valley of the Hammocks.

Grandpa Melendez was a respected dentist whose patients included some of San Salvador's commercial, industrial, financial, and cultural leaders. His offices were in the front rooms of the large Melendez home.

A typical upper-middle-class home inside, its large rooms contained furniture of handcarved wood; colorful tapestries hung on the walls between old oil paintings and framed black-and-white photos of the family. The building looked more like a fortress from the outside, however, with cement walls rising six feet above the sidewalk and topped with twelve more feet of wood covered with corrugated iron. A huge, rather ornate doorway fronted on the sidewalk; behind that, a small inner door led into a courtyard.

The dental offices, a waiting room, the living quarters of the Melendez family, Grandpa's personal office, the library, several spare bedrooms, the dining room, the kitchen, and the maid's quarters all surrounded an open, red-and-blue-tiled courtyard with an ornate marble fountain and a pool of water. Trees, bougainvillea vines, orchids in pots, and beds of flowers were open to the sky. Parakeets and wild parrots darted about the courtyard—flocks of them.

The courtyard and surrounding hallways were big enough to field a family soccer match, but we never tried it. That's not Grandpa Melendez's style. We didn't even dare sneak into the kitchen for a late-night snack, because anyone caught red-handed (or red-footed, in my case) was booted out. And we never mixed with the servants. In Rivas, Grandma's hired help was part of the family, but Grandpa Melendez believed in the separation of the classes.

Grandpa was a handsome old man with long, elegant hands and fingers, silver-gray hair, a stern but friendly face, and eyes that twinkled when he was pleased. Grandma was delicate, petite, and rather noble in her bearing. She spoke quietly, yet her word was law to us children and to the servants. My grandparents loved our family, but there was still a distance between us.

The whole Melendez family, like its patriarch, was rather dispassionate. Men didn't cry—at least not in public—and women, though honored and cared for, were expected to keep within the traditional limits of their roles as wife, mother, and keeper of the home.

It wasn't easy to know the private side of a Melendez. My father never talked to us children about money, sex, Christian faith, or the personal problems he or we might be having. We were pretty much left alone in that regard—or left to Mother.

Looking back, it's easy to see how much my father resembled his father. Each loved as well as he could love, but each suffered silently and alone.

THE DESTRUCTION OF MANAGUA

Two days before Christmas in 1972, our family lay sleeping in Grandpa and Grandma Melendez's home. Having recently completed the long journey from our little house in Chino, we were happy to have had a real bath, some wonderful homecooked meals, and several nights in soft featherbeds. It was past midnight when Grandpa woke us up, looking terribly worried. Dad and he conferred for a moment in the hallway, Dad still half-asleep as Grandpa began to whisper in his ear. Suddenly my father gasped.

"Wake up, everybody," he said, as if we weren't already awake. "Get packed. We're leaving!"

I was just ten years old, but I still remember how frightened my mother looked as Grandpa repeated to all of us what he had just heard on the radio.

"There was an earthquake," he said, "centered on Lake Nicaragua near Managua. The capital is burning and in ruins. Thousands of people have died. Tens of thousands are hurt and homeless. We can't find out anything yet about Rivas or your family there."

My father tried to telephone Rivas while we were packing, but not even an operator came on the line. Managua and Rivas were built along the same "circle of fire," a ring of volcanoes and seismic fault lines that encircles the Pacific Ocean from the Aleutians down through the western rim of the Americas to New Zealand and up through Japan.

Managua is thus disaster-prone. Destroyed completely in 1885 and then again in 1931, the capital of Nicaragua is terribly vulnerable to earthquakes. My grandparents had told us about living through the 1931 quake that killed 1,450 people in Managua alone. We didn't know what had happened in Rivas, and the only way to find out was by going there.

Dad drove us nonstop through southern El Salvador, the southern tip of Honduras, and León, the second-largest city in Nicaragua, to the outskirts of Managua.

"*Alto!*" the sign read simply. "Do not proceed!"

Dad ran up to the police barricade blocking traffic into the capital. "I *must* enter," he said. "I have family who need me."

The police officers tried to explain to my father that Managua wasn't safe to enter. Down near the shores of Lake Nicaragua the earth had swallowed buildings, cars, buses, and the people trapped inside. Avenida Central, in the heart of the city, was completely leveled. Most of the restaurants, office buildings, shops, and homes in that area were seriously damaged if not destroyed. The hospital at which doctors had operated on my clubfoot was in ruins. Three hundred and twenty square blocks of the city were designated a "contaminated area," and whole blocks of buildings were still in flames.

And though the world was mobilizing to send food and supplies to the broken city, the real problem was the bands of looters who swooped down upon Managua to steal everything they could carry. Even as people dug desperately through ruined buildings to unbury friends and family, a veritable war broke out between the looters, whom General Somoza called "abominable beings," and the police and army units he had sent to drive them away.

Frustrated, and growing more and more afraid, my father turned back from the police barricade and drove until he found an unbarricaded road leading into the city. As we drove through Managua, no one spoke. I remember staring out the rear window at houses with the roof gone and walls collapsed. I could see people stumbling through the debris and digging in the piles of brick and broken timber. Most were looking for people they loved who might be buried there. I saw bodies piled up in parks and in open spaces along the road. Six thousand men, women, and children had died, and to protect the living from disease, city officials were pouring gasoline on the dead and burning them where they had expired.

We learned later that the epicenter of the major quake was just nine miles beneath the earth's surface almost directly below Managua. And because the city was built on volcanic debris and not solid rock, even a small quake would have threatened to destroy it.

There was no way to find family or friends who needed help in Managua. Most streets and alleys were blocked by piles of debris. Police and army barricades were everywhere. Telephone communications had been destroyed. The Red Cross was only beginning to draw up long lists of the injured and the dead.

So we drove directly to Rivas. Grandpa and Grandma embraced us tearfully. Their home had received only minor damage from the quake, but many of their friends and colleagues had lost everything. I remember wandering around the house, watching the grownups whisper back and forth about the tragedy. Grandma sat in silence, fingering her rosary and praying for the dead.

Grandpa, my father, and José drove back to Managua several times in the days that followed to search for friends and family and to help alleviate the suffering in any way they could. I played with my Uncle Gerardo and my sisters. It wasn't exactly a time for fun and games. Still, the adults could think only about death and dying, and as the days past, I grew bored.

One afternoon I wandered down to a little stream at the edge of Rivas, carrying over my shoulder the bucket my brother used for catching frogs. He was away with my dad in Managua at the time. I decided that if José could catch those slimy little critters with his hands and fingers, I could catch them just as well with my feet and toes. I lay on my back near an unsuspecting target. Then, with a quick jab of my right foot and a scooping motion with my left, I flung it into the bucket so fast it didn't know what had happened. Before an hour had passed, I had a bucketful of frogs for my family. I knew that they would be pleased.

Grandma Rodriquez was the first to see me marching up from the creek looking like a creature from the lost lagoon. In her excitement to get me into the bathtub, the bucket spilled and frogs flopped everywhere. Several months after our return to Chino, Grandpa called from Rivas with the news that they had had to hire a professional to capture and cart away the community of frogs that had developed in, around, and under their home in Rivas.

On our last weekend in Nicaragua, my father took us down to Lake Nicaragua for a picnic and a swim. I was swimming on my back with my sisters and Uncle Gerardo when I felt something bite the little "finger" that sticks out of my left shoulder.

I screamed and jumped up out of the water, but when I explained what had happened, everybody laughed and made jokes about piranha and tiny little sharks that picked on me only. But the minute I went back into the water, fish began to chew on me again. This time blood dripped down my side from the wounds the fish had made. Everybody saw the bright-red stream flowing from my injury into the clear water. All the joking about sharks and piranha stopped suddenly as everybody joined me on the beach.

All our activities that trip were permeated with the Christmas spirit. Christmas in Rivas is different from Christmas in America. In America people think mainly of buying presents and of eating turkey and pumpkin pies together. But in Rivas Christmas is a time for attending worship, praying for the world, and celebrating the birth of Jesus, our Lord.

I'll never forget that Christmas in Rivas, just two days after the 1972 earthquake that destroyed Managua and killed thousands of people. The midnight mass was dedicated to those who had died in that terrible quake. Our cathedral was filled to overflowing. The altars were ablaze with candles burning in memory of the dead. I don't remember receiving or giving gifts that year; I don't remember decorations or parties or celebrations. I just remember kneeling between my grandpa and my grandma in that great church and listening to the sound of the people crying softly or praying. Heads were bowed and eyes were closed, but I sneaked a peek at the candle shadows dancing on the walls and ceilings. They looked like angels.

From my earliest childhood Mom had told me that God is with us in times of light and times of darkness. I felt him close that day, weeping with us for those who suffered and for those who had died. Little did I know that day about the times of darkness just ahead for me and my family, or the light that God would bring to see us through.

9. The Junior High Years

Seeing the dead and dying people in the streets of Managua helped speed up my journey from childhood to adolescence. I went to Central America that winter as a sixth-grade kid; I came back to the United States having been forced to grow up, at least a little. So when my parents and the teachers at Cypress Orthopedic School decided that I should stay at Cypress instead of graduating into a public junior high school, I was angry and disappointed.

I didn't feel handicapped. I wanted to be accepted as just another kid on the block. I wanted to learn my own lessons, to make my own mistakes. Win or lose, I wanted to fight my own battles without being rescued just because I had no arms.

"Let me try!" I begged my brother one afternoon as he stood in the center of a ring of neighborhood children playing Ball in the Basket.

"Later, Tony," he said, passing the ball to a boy from down the street.

"Not later," I protested. "*Now!*"

José was the neighborhood champion at Ball in the Basket. You've probably seen the tools of the trade: a small wooden cup at the end of a smooth stick, to which a hard rubber ball is attached by a cord. The object is to swing the ball so that it lands in the little cup. It takes a swift hand and a sharp eye to get that ball into place, but I was determined to do with my feet anything my brother or his friends could do with their hands.

"Tony," my brother said, leaning down to whisper in my ear, "you can't do it!"

For a moment I glared at him. I hated it when anybody told me what I could or couldn't do, even politely. José was just trying to keep me from being embarrassed—I knew that even then—but it still made me angry. As he turned to rejoin his friends, I lowered my right shoulder and charged into him like a battering ram.

José stumbled over another child and fell to the ground, yelling in surprise and hurt. I fled toward the front door of our little house in Chino with José after me. I kicked open the screendoor and ran into the kitchen, José gaining rapidly.

"Mom!" I shouted. "Mom!"

José had me pinned to the kitchen floor when Mother entered from her bedroom, and I was kicking and screaming for help. She separated us, scolded José, and sent him back outside. Then she turned to me.

"I want to play Ball in the Basket," I said. "José won't let me."

Mom knew immediately what had happened. We had been through this same routine so many times before. For a moment she stared at me, shaking her head slowly and grinning her tired grin. Then she walked silently into the living room and out the front door. I followed at a distance, wondering what she was going to do.

"José," my mother said, walking up to the children still playing in the middle of our front yard, "when it's time, let Tony have his turn."

"But Mom, Tony can't . . ."

"You heard me," Mom answered firmly. "Let Tony have his turn."

José groaned. The other children looked at me: a boy with no arms insisting on his turn at Ball in the Basket. Their eyes said it all; and how I hated that look of pity. Let me try, even if I fail. Please at least let me try.

"Your turn," José said gruffly, tossing the stick to the ground at my feet. I wedged the smooth handle between my toes and began to swing the ball in a little arc. Then, with a twist of my ankle, I tossed the ball upward toward the mouth of the cup. The ball bounced off the lip of the cup and dangled at my feet again.

"Nice try, Tony," a neighbor girl said.

I hated hearing those words almost as much as I hated the look of pity that usually went with them.

Pity, even well-meant pity, hurts far more than it helps. I wanted the kids to shut up and wait while I took my turn just as they shut up and waited for everybody else. I didn't mind if they groaned or snickered when I missed—or even laughed at my awkward and unsuccessful first attempts at Ball in the Basket—but I didn't want pity. Pity says, "You aren't one of us." Pity says, "We'll make new rules for you." Pity says, "We can never really be your friend."

Laugh at me. Ridicule me. Knock me down and sit on my head. But don't pity me.

"Tony," José said quietly, "your turn is up. Pass the game to Peter."

I still had the stick grasped between my toes, and I continued to swing the ball more and more frantically, trying to get it to land in that elusive cup. But after the first try, I hadn't even managed to hit the lip of the cup again. I was missing by a mile.

"Tony," José said again, and this time his patience had run out, "give me that thing."

I backed off with the stick still wedged between my toes. When José moved to follow, I flung the game at him with a quick twist of my ankle and ran back toward the house. This time José just shrugged and walked down Essex Street with his friends in tow. I stood behind the screendoor watching them walk away. The stick lay abandoned on the rutted front lawn. For a moment I felt sorry for myself. Then I kicked open the screendoor, walked up to the stick, and grasped it between my toes once again.

"Get in there," I said, swinging the ball with a hard upward thrust of my ankle. "Land in the cup!"

I missed again. And again and again. No matter what I did, the ball would *not* go in. My mother remembers that I sat there for more than an hour working at it. Finally she came out with a glass of lemonade and sat down beside me. Angry and determined, I kept on tossing the ball up into the air. Each time it fell short of the cup or bounced in and out immediately.

"Tony," Mom said suddenly, "you've blistered two of your toes. Look: the skin is worn away, and one toe is starting to bleed."

I scooted away from her with the ball still swinging up, missing, and swinging up again.

"Tony, you have to stop," Mom finally ordered, reaching down to take the game away.

I tried to run, but she grabbed me from behind. I was shaking. For a moment she held me in her arms, though I tried to pull away.

"It's all right, Tony," she said. "You'll do it, in time. But you have to let me bandage the blisters."

I practiced that stupid game so long and so often that my mother eventually had to hide it from me during meals and study time. I blistered almost every toe in the process of wedging, twisting, tossing, endlessly practicing—until one day the ball dropped into the cup!

I looked down at the rubber ball lying trapped and defeated in its hollow little bowl. I had won. I was afraid to move for fear that the ball would bounce out and that I would never get it back into the cup again. Then slowly I tipped the cup, and the ball dangled from its cord. I tossed it into the air and—miracle of miracles—the ball dropped into the cup a second time.

"Tony, you did it!" my mother said, rushing up to me from behind.

She says that I didn't even look up at her or smile or take a well-deserved break. I just kept swinging the ball into the air and into the cup until I had the trick mastered. My toes were all covered with bandages, and my feet didn't really heal for several weeks. But let me tell you, the next time that circle of neighborhood friends stood in my front yard, I was there in the middle of them, insisting on my turn.

THE END OF THE MECHANICAL ARM

My legs and ankles, my feet and toes grew strong and skillful during my elementary and junior high school years in Chino. The therapists at Cypress Orthopedic School made me use my mechanical arm for years. They even got an experimental electric second arm for me to try, complete with batteries, motors, and little buzzing sounds. But I hated those arms and continued hiding or losing them as often as I could.

"I can get by with my feet," I told the therapist.

"But you'll need arms," she insisted, "if not now, in the future. And to use your arms skillfully when you do need them, you must practice with them now."

Call me stubborn if you want. (My parents did, regularly.) Or call me lazy. (One of the therapists at Cypress did so in front of the whole class.) Or call me stupid and short-sighted. (I could see that judgment in many people's eyes.) But I refused to use those arms, and one day everybody quit trying to force me into it.

I think I was thirteen when they put away the arm forever. One day the therapist, coming at me with that plastic-and-steel contraption, took one look at my frowning, determined face, sighed in exasperation, turned back into her office, and put the arm up on the shelf. That same arm still hangs on the wall of our garage, a kind of grisly memorial to what might have been.

Finally, after ten years of trying, my therapist and my parents gave up. They knew that I had grown perfectly competent to get by in life with no arms, real or mechanical. In fact, I had just won the Cypress Orthopedic School snooker championship, playing against all those kids with real arms. I could wedge the regulation-sized pool cue between my chin and shoulder, lean down across the table, and hit the ball cleanly and accurately without digging into the green-felt table or toppling over onto my face.

I couldn't use a bicycle, but I could flip a skateboard onto my shoulder, walk to the nearest sidewalk, and glide noiselessly to almost anyplace in Chino or its environs.

I couldn't throw a football, but I competed every year in the mini-Olympics that Cypress Orthopedic School staged for their "handi-capable" students, and I won my share of blue ribbons in every event from the four-person relay to the ladder climb.

I couldn't play the violin or trumpet, but I soon discovered that there was at least one instrument that I could play. Dad had bought an electronic organ at a garage sale. I later found it in his bedroom, wedged it between my chin and shoulder, carried it to school, and learned to play it with my toes.

And I could swim like a fish. Actually, swimming began for me in our bathtub in Rivas soon after I was born. Mom used to fill the small tub until it threatened to overflow. She remembers laying me in the tub on my back with her hand holding my head above the water.

"One day you just floated away from me," she remembers. "You were kicking, rotating your shoulders, and moving through the water backwards when you were less than eighteen inches long."

THE FAMILY POOL

Chino was almost fifty miles from the ocean. But on Saturdays, if we had enough money to pay for the extra tank of gas, Dad drove us to the beach at Newport, Huntington Beach, or Long Beach. Mom packed a huge lunch (so we wouldn't pester her to buy hamburgers and fries from the expensive beachfront fast-food chains), and Dad loaded the car with blankets, games, a beach umbrella, and folding chairs.

"It's too bad we don't have a pool," my mom said one day as we were driving back from Huntington Beach.

Everybody was surprised to hear Mom talk wistfully about having a swimming pool. My dad and mom were both working for close to minimum wage, sometimes two full jobs a day, and we still couldn't pay the bills. We were on welfare, and we used food stamps. We often bought our clothing at the swap meet. It was a shock that my mother, of all people, would even joke about having a swimming pool.

A pool in Los Angeles was a major luxury. To have a house with a pool was beyond our wildest dreams. One of our neighbors had a portable, above-ground Dough Boy plastic pool in their back yard, but we were never invited to swim in it. On hot summer days, or in the spring or fall after school and on the weekends, we would walk by that pool and wish that we had one in our own back yard. But until Mom planted the idea in Dad's mind, we never imagined that we would have a pool of our very own.

Then one Saturday my dad and his brother pulled into our back yard carrying on the back of my uncle's truck the neighbor's Dough Boy pool.

"Chelle," my mother shouted excitedly, running out the back, "that's the neighbor's pool."

For a moment I thought my father had stolen it. Despite the biblical warnings, we had all coveted our neighbor's pool, wishing it into our back yard. But then I realized that my father was too honest to steal even a paperclip from the bank or an extra paper bag from the grocery store.

"Help me unload this thing," Dad yelled, pointing at the pile of metal siding and plastic on the back of the truck.

José, Mayella, Mom, and even Marylou began to help drag the huge pool liner off the truck bed.

"Pile it there," Dad said, pointing to a spot in the middle of the back yard near five large bags of sand. "First we need to spread the sand. Then we have to get the frame in place."

It took about an hour to shovel and smooth the sand, to pound the stakes, and to fix into place the round metal walls of the above-ground pool.

"Okay," Dad said when the walls were anchored, "let's straighten up the lining and pull it into place."

As we stretched the lining up over the walls, we noticed that the blue-and-green plastic was pockmarked with tiny holes. Then we discovered that there were several rather large rips in the plastic as well.

"This won't hold water," José said quietly to my father.

"That's why the neighbors gave it to me," Dad said, grinning.

Nobody took the risk of betting against my father's determination. After we straightened and scrubbed the plastic walls, Dad produced a plastic patching kit and went to work. José and Mayella helped cut and place the patches, and I sat on them to be sure that they would hold. By early evening the patches were dry.

"Let's fill it up," Dad said, moving the garden hose into place.

By then friends and neighbors were gathering for the opening of the new Melendez pool. There were burgers on the barbecue and cold drinks in the little ice chest. I had slipped into my bathing suit hours before and was waiting patiently for the patches to dry. Even once the pool was filled, nobody was sure that it would hold. Mom remembers worrying that the back yard, the garage, and even the house might end up flooded when the patches gave way. But the look of excitement and determination in my father's eyes kept everyone silent about their fears.

"See, Saruca?" my dad said proudly to Mom. "You wanted a pool: we have a pool."

Dad took my mother by the hand and led her up the well-used steps into our newly patched pool. Everybody cheered when she stepped into the water. "It's cold!" she yelled, jumping out again.

But that didn't stop the rest of us; we all charged into the pool together. Mom says that I looked like a dolphin circling the pool under water, twisting my body and kicking my feet to pick up speed.

"Every few laps you would thrust your head up out of the water," Mom said. "You would catch your shoulder on the edge of the pool and rest there, grinning as you watched everyone else playing in the pool. Your eyes would sparkle. Then you'd take a deep breath and dive head-first into the pool again for another under-water lap."

Even in junior high school I was developing a strong neck and torso. I could race around the pool like a dolphin, as Mom had observed. I could even carry my little sisters—one at a time—on my back as I swam above and below the waterline. I could dive too. I just stood on the little platform above the pool and launched myself into the air.

We patched and pampered our neighbor's discarded pool into years of service to our family. It was the largest and finest of our recycling efforts, but it wasn't the first. We were poor, after all. I think it's hard for most people to understand just how poor an American immigrant family can be. And when there's no money for food, there's no money for fun. So you improvise.

HAVING FUN FOR FREE

The Melendez family became quite skilled at having fun for free. We children made dirt pizzas, for example, and covered them with every imaginable (and often disgusting) kind of topping. A sprinkle of grass for cheese or a handful of pebbles for pepperoni—Marylou didn't care. She was our taster. At five years old, she would eat anything.

Now and then one of our generous relatives would stop by at Christmas or on a birthday with a new expensive toy with an electrical motor and moving parts, but Dad and Mom made sure we also had plenty of second-hand toys—dolls, puzzles, balls, board games, trucks, and cars—to play with. We might not have had the famous brand names being advertised like kids today have computer toys or the Cabbage Patch Kids, but our used, generic versions were just as entertaining.

I remember finding an old plastic hula hoop in a neighbor's trash pile. I carried it home over my shoulder and mastered it in a weekend. That hula hoop may have been headed for the city dump when I found it, but it had at least three more years of life by the time I taught Mayella and Marylou how to keep it spinning.

When neighbor children were going to the movies, to a concert, or to a Dodgers game, we stayed home and improvised. We saw most of the movies six months after their release on our used black-and-white television set, and the concerts and the games usually ended up on the radio or on a tape we could bootleg from a friend.

When neighbor kids vacationed in Hawaii, we used our Dough Boy pool to snorkel or to treasure-hunt. We concealed costume jewelry beneath rocks on the bottom of the pool and dove for that and other buried treasures. We staged swimming Olympics, pirate attacks, and naval wars. We had our own private resort in the back yard of the little house on Essex Street, and especially on weekends our house and the patched pool echoed with the laughter of our family and our friends.

WEEKENDS ON ESSEX STREET

Dad was the real spirit behind our weekend adventures. We were poor but we seldom noticed, because Dad helped to fill our lives with excitement. We didn't see him much during the week, but he always saved some time for us on the weekends.

"Let's get out of here," Dad would shout, heading us toward the door early on a Saturday morning.

"Wait," Mom would say, leading Mayella and Marylou into the kitchen to finish up the picnic lunch that she was packing. Somehow, Mom always got a huge lunch into the ice chest just in time for Dad's adventures.

In the summer Dad might drive us to Redondo Beach to swim and picnic, to window-shop in the wonderful little stores and galleries on the pier, to play volleyball in the sand, and at the end of the day to roast marshmallows over a campfire and watch the sun sink below the distant Pacific horizon.

On winter days Dad might drive us to a swap meet or to a neighborhood garage sale. He would give us each a dollar—and two hours to spend it. We would race up and down the rows of goodies, searching for the bargain of the century; and then race back, purchase in hand, to win Dad's smiling approval.

Mount Baldy and the range of mountains that rise up behind Los Angeles can go several years without a real snowstorm. But on those rare southern California days when the evergreen trees were bent with white, Dad loved to drive us into the mountains for an adventure in the snow. We usually brought cardboard, smoothed and waterproofed with candle wax, for sledding, although sometimes Dad brought used inner tubes or garbage-can lids.

Mom remembers one run in particular. She says that I was nine or ten years old at the time. On previous runs I had ridden down the hill between my father's legs, held in place on the makeshift sled by his arms around me.

"This time I want to do it alone," I begged at the top of the hill. Dad paused. Mom shouted warnings. Too late. Dad pushed me over the edge of the sled run, and suddenly—sitting by myself on the heavily waxed slick cardboard—I found myself moving faster every second. Without arms or hands, there was absolutely no way I could hang on, so I tried hard to balance as the cardboard sled careened down the steep hillside. I saw a rise looming ahead but had no way to steer around it.

"You went up in the air," Mom said, "like an unguided missile. The cardboard continued down the hill as you rose toward the trees. And when you fell back to earth, you landed on your head and then began to roll like a log straight down the mountain."

Apparently I was rolling—screaming and laughing simultaneously—when I hit a large boulder and wrapped myself around it. No bones were broken; only my pride suffered from the fall. I still remember the excitement of that ride: the sudden launching into space, the rough return to earth, the long, freezing roll in the snow, and the sudden stop near the end of the trail.

And above all the other sounds that accompany that memory, I can still hear my mother's warning, "Tony, be careful!" and my father's loud reply, "Atta boy, Tony. Atta boy!"

10. The Senior High Years

"Tony?"

My ninth-grade English teacher was trying to get my attention. It wasn't easy. Attentiveness wasn't my strong suit. As a result, my freshman year at Ontario High School was a disaster—at least most of it was a disaster.

"Tony!"

I had been a student at Cypress Orthopedic School for five of my elementary school years and for both years of junior high school.

"Tony!!"

When I entered high school as a ninth-grader, I wanted to be in "normal" classes with "normal" students. Instead, I was enrolled in the handicapped program at Ontario High with my old friends from Cypress Orthopedic. Meeting in special classrooms equipped for the handicapped, and taught by the same two teachers in all the subjects, we were largely cut off from the other kids. We even had P.E. classes for the handicapped, in which we pushed shuffleboard markers and played paper-and-pencil games.

"Tony!!!"

My exasperated teacher was now leaning down over my desk and practically shouting in my ear. She had been trying to get my attention for the past five weeks. It wasn't working. Finally I looked back at her with my meanest look. It scared my sisters. Why wouldn't it scare her?

"You'd better get me out of this class," I said slowly, leaving just enough space between each word to make the sentence sound angry, almost threatening. "And you'd better get me into a *normal* high school program," I added, "because I'm going nuts here. I can't stand it any longer."

For a moment she stared down at me in silence. I wasn't a disorderly kid—at least not most of the time. But my patience had run out. I was just fourteen years old, and yet I was confronting my teacher head-on. Worse, there was a slight chance that she would take my wider complaint rather personally, when in fact she was a good teacher, and well aware of my dilemma.

"Oh, Tony," she said quietly, sitting down in the empty desk beside me and scribbling a note on her little pad. "What are we going to do with you?" I wondered that too.

Don't misunderstand me. Handicapped classes can be excellent. And teachers of the handicapped are loving and very patient. But because there isn't usually money to hire adequate staff or to create small, specialized classes for each achievement level, the classes and the teachers have to move slowly, pacing themselves to the slowest student's ability to learn. At that pace I would have had a high school education in half a century.

To make matters worse, emotionally handicapped students sat side by side with the educationally and physically handicapped. Again because of inadequate budgets, we were all lumped together. I had no arms, but I was normal in every other way. I wanted to be with normal kids, and finally this poor teacher understood.

"Okay, Tony," she whispered, "I'll try again. Take this note to the counselor. See what he can do."

I was so excited that I jumped up out of my desk and raced for the door without looking back.

AT LAST I'M NORMAL!

"This is Coach Thompson," the counselor said, introducing me to my new P.E. teacher. "Coach, this kid begged to be in your class," he added, grinning. "Make it miserable for him."

Both men laughed. The counselor patted me on the shoulder and wished me well before returning to his office.

I had worked hard to convince him—to convince *everybody*—that arms or no arms, I could make it in the real world. At last somebody had taken me seriously. The counselors had decided that

I would stay in certain courses for the handicapped but that I would take regular gym classes and have a chance to prove myself in regular freshman English.

The coach led me to the locker room. Out of the corner of my eye, I could see that my presence stunned him, at least temporarily. The coaching staff had never had a gym student with no arms—let alone a stubborn one determined to play intramural soccer.

"Do you need help suiting up, Tony?" the coach asked.

"No help, Coach," I answered a bit defensively. "I can do it myself."

The moment he left the locker room, I began to scramble into gym pants, a regulation T-shirt, and tennis shoes. It wasn't easy, and I followed him into the large gymnasium with my shirt dangling and my shoes unlaced. Long lines of "normal" teenage boys were lined up for calisthenics. They were talking, laughing, and punching each other affectionately when I appeared. All at once the room, which had echoed with their voices, grew unnaturally quiet.

"This is Tony," the coach announced. "He'll be playing soccer with us for the next four weeks."

I walked to the end of the line. Fifty mouths dropped open, speechless. Fifty pairs of eyes followed me.

"Thirty jumping jacks," the coach said, blowing his whistle for attention. "One, two; one, two; one, two!"

One hundred arms were swinging back and forth. One hundred voices were counting in unison. And one hundred eyes were trying hard not to look in my direction.

I knew what they were thinking: how does a guy with no arms do a jumping jack? I grinned. This was the beginning of a new life for me. After what I had been through, jumping jacks were no sweat. I jumped up and down, swinging my invisible arms and shouting the count so that everyone could hear. "One, two; one, two; one, two!"

It took only eight or ten counts before the guys began to grin at me.

"Okay, *Tony!*" someone shouted as we neared the end of the

count. It was a welcome to the real world that I wouldn't forget. I was in a normal class at last! I would prove to this normal teacher and to his normal students that I could play soccer with the best of them.

The next day I was transferred to a normal English class as well. The word was out. I was making the crossing; I was becoming one of the normal guys. You just don't know how good that feels until you've been seen as abnormal most of your life. Maybe that's why I don't like people to get all excited about all the things I can do with my feet and toes. It makes me feel abnormal all over again.

Actually, you could do the same things I do with your feet and toes if you had no hands or fingers. I had to teach myself skills that you don't need but that you could master if the need arose. Anyway, it felt (and it still feels) good to be accepted as normal, to have nobody notice or gasp or turn away when I walked into a room.

It took time, however. The next morning, when I walked into my new English class, all eyes were fixed on me. I hated that. The bell rang, and the teacher went to the board and began to lecture. Taking an unclaimed seat, I shrugged off my backpack, unzipped it, and pulled out a pencil and a notebook with my toes. Even the teacher stared at me as I toed open my notebook, grasped the stubby pencil between my two biggest toes, and began to take notes on paper on the floor at my feet.

There was silence. I looked up, knowing why the teacher had stopped her discussion of Herman Melville's *Moby Dick* in the middle of a sentence. Nobody spoke; they all just stared at me. Somebody had to break the silence.

"Hope the floor is clean," I said, grinning just slightly. "If it isn't, I'll have to turn in a dirty paper."

The class roared. The teacher joined in the laughter and then began her lecture once again. My poor little toes were writing like mad, but I could hardly hear what the woman was saying; my heart was beating too loudly. I had made my move: I would never see myself as handicapped again.

THE SOPHOMORE SCRAMBLE

Unfortunately, during the high school years that followed there were teachers and students who needed convincing that a young man with no arms was really normal.

"Hurry, Tony," José yelled, looking back over his shoulder as he helped me scramble for my sophomore classes. After I had made it in several normal classes at Ontario High School, Dad and Mom agreed that I could register in the fall at Chino High, my hometown high school. My big brother, who was a junior at Chino, knew the ropes and had volunteered to help me enroll.

"You want this English teacher," he whispered as we neared the front of the line. "Believe me," he added, "the other guy's a dog."

I had tried to tell José that I could scramble for classes by myself, but he had insisted on helping me.

"There are piles of cards to fill out," he said, "and dozens of teachers to choose between. You have to run from line to line trying to get the best ones, or you'll end up in dog city!"

We raced across the campus and stood with dozens of other students in a line that ended at a popular teacher's desk.

"Is this card for you?" she said, holding out the registration form to José.

"No," he answered honestly, "it's for my brother, Tony."

She followed his glance in my direction. Then she paused and lowered the card. Her smile didn't change. There was no special look in her eyes, no gesture that gave away exactly what she was thinking.

"I'm sorry," she said, "I can't enroll your brother in this class."

Nobody in our family takes "no" very well, and José can be tougher than any of us. He leaned down across her table, reached for the card, and began to make my case.

"I'm sorry, no," she said, totally unpersuaded by my brother's pleas.

"What a jerk," José whispered to me when another student interrupted with a question.

Looking back now, we both understand why she hesitated. Public school teachers, with classes that are too large, have no extra money budgeted for special personnel, books, or equipment. And this was an honors class. She wanted students who could race ahead of the pack. She didn't want to penalize the bright, hard-working, college-bound kids by enrolling somebody who might hold them back—even if that somebody was I.

"Tony is bright," José said, exaggerating just a little. "He can keep up, don't worry!"

"I'm sorry," the teacher repeated, ending the argument that had grown quite heated. "Next student, please."

José refused to turn away, however. His voice was a bit too loud as he made one last attempt on my behalf. Hearing the commotion, a tall, distinguished-looking man in a charcoal-brown suit and matching tie walked over to the frustrated teacher and leaned down to whisper in her ear. José stood back from the table and looked away discreetly. The teacher, turning red with anger, began to respond. Noticing the crowd of students all turned in their direction, the tall man led the teacher toward the shade of a tree just outside the door.

"That's the principal," José said, grinning with triumph. "He'll tell her what's what!"

We watched the teacher and the principal arguing out under the tree. She was obviously frustrated, while he was cool and quiet. She gestured and spoke rapidly. He listened, spoke briefly, listened again, and then walked away. The teacher turned slowly and walked back into the room. She sat at her desk, picked up the registration card, and held it out to me.

"Good luck," she said, "to both of us."

I grasped the card in my teeth, then bent my neck and dropped the card into my shirt pocket without missing a beat.

"Not bad," she said, grinning a tired grin that made me know that everything would be all right, if I came through. And I did come through. Before the semester ended, we were good friends. I'm glad that José held his ground against that teacher's fear, and before the year was over, that teacher was glad as well.

ON BEING NORMAL

During those three years at Chino High, I proved to almost everybody that I was normal. One Friday night at a Chino High football game, I sat with a group of sophomores who had opened up their circle of friendship and let me in.

"I'm going to the snack bar," a tall blond girl said quietly during the second quarter. "Anything I can get you?"

"Yes," I said, "pizza!"

"Pizza?" she repeated—wondering, I suppose, how I would eat it.

"Yup," I repeated, "pizza: deep-dish pizza with extra cheese, Canadian bacon, smoked ham, spicy pepperoni, and Italian sausage."

"Don't get your hopes up," she said, grinning and shaking her head. "This is junior-class volunteer pizza, remember? But I'll see what I can find."

I didn't even think to go with her. My brother was on the field at the time. He started for both Chino's offensive and its defensive teams. We were a small school, but José was one good athlete; and I didn't want to miss a move he made.

That night even my mom and dad, who didn't understand football, were in the stands, sitting nearby. They came to cheer José, although with everybody dressed the same, Mom and Dad couldn't even recognize him on the field. And not understanding the rules or the announcer's rapid patter, they sat silently in the bleachers, looking at the confusing jumble of bodies and waiting to hear the name Melendez. Then they cheered.

I was proud of my big brother and enjoyed bragging about him to my small but growing group of friends. I secretly wanted to be out there on the field myself, however, hearing my parents and my friends cheering for me too.

"Here it is," the blond girl said, sitting down beside me and opening a box of football pizza: thin, burned crust, hard, stringy cheese, and wilted tomato slices. She got the pizza box open in her lap and then paused and looked confused. Before she could say,

"Well, what do we do now?" I dropped my face into the box, snared a healthy piece of pizza with my teeth and tongue, and began to eat it.

"Oh, my gosh," she said, "look at you."

We shared the pizza that night, but then she disappeared back into the crowd. It often happened that way. Girls would take me on as a project, then just disappear. I didn't blame them. Who would want a boyfriend with no arms? I began to think that I could prove myself normal in most ways but never really be seen as normal by the girls.

So I stayed away from the school dances that were held in the high school gymnasium on occasional Friday or Saturday nights. Class officers and volunteers decorated the gym with streamers and colorful set-pieces. The kids wore formals and rented tuxedos, and a few of the wealthy couples even arrived in rented limousines. Usually disc jockeys played tapes through large stereo speakers, but occasionally live bands were hired to perform. But I stayed home, watched television, and felt miserable.

I knew that I could dance well enough, but I was afraid that I would scare the girls away. I didn't want to become an object of pity again. And I hated the idea of standing against the wall alone until some girl took me on as a charity case before retiring me to the wall again. But Mayella and Marylou both encouraged me to take the chance.

"High school girls aren't fussy," Mayella teased me. "There'll be at least one of them who's desperate enough to ask you to dance."

I went to my first dance without a date. Just as in my nightmare, I ended up standing alone against the back wall of the gym. Contrary to my nightmare, however, I didn't mind standing there. The lights were low, the music was loud, and the dancers moved in and out of the splashes of light made by the spotlights and lasers turning just overhead. It was fun to watch them, but I remember feeling a little uncomfortable, wondering if I should ask someone to dance or if someone would eventually ask me.

All of a sudden one of the girls from my English class walked up to me, looked me in the eye impatiently, and said, "Go!" It was obvious that she wanted me to dance with her. Her approach wasn't very romantic, but seconds later we were tearing up the floor, and I've been dancing almost nonstop ever since.

THE HOPE-GIVERS

I don't think that girl will ever know how important she was to me that night. At various times in my life people like her have come along to say or do just the right thing when I needed it. These sensitive ones are the hope-givers. They're rare, because they can get their minds off their own problems long enough to reach out to help someone else in need.

My lockermate, Paolo, a sophomore from Brazil, was another hope-giver I met that first year at Chino High School. There was no way I could work the combination on my rusty high school locker. Paolo saw me struggling with it one day and asked if he could help. From that moment on, he was always almost magically there beside me to help get my locker opened and my books in and out on time.

One afternoon in late fall Paolo brought me hope in yet another way. In our conversations at the locker and during lunch, he realized how much I wanted to be on an athletic team.

"Why don't you try out for soccer?" he asked me. "You don't need arms for soccer. You use your head and feet and legs."

I hadn't even told him that I had played intramural soccer in my freshman P.E. class at Ontario High, or that I had gotten through two seasons of neighborhood soccer action. I don't know why I kept that little secret to myself. I suppose that getting to play soccer at all—even with neighborhood kids or my fellow freshmen—was an achievement that I didn't want to risk by being turned down for the high school team.

"Tryouts are tomorrow," Paolo said, "and you're coming with me whether you like it or not."

Paolo, the hope-giver, promised to help me into soccer shoes and a uniform for the tryouts, and I promised to appear. I wandered onto the field on the appointed day feeling unafraid but rather sheepish. Many members of the Chino team had been playing soccer for years. For some of them, getting a place on that team was their most important high school goal.

The coach looked in my direction, paused for just a split second, then blew his whistle to get us into line. We were divided into teams to scrimmage against each other. Coaches and volunteer scouts wandered up and down the field, watching us play. Obviously an armless soccer player brings some disadvantages to his team. But I could get to the ball faster than the fastest of them. The coaches and scouts watched in amazement as I ran up and down the field using my head, my legs, and my feet to keep the ball in play.

When the final whistle blew, I hadn't scored, nor had I made any miracle plays. But I had run fast and hustled hard. I could see the coach writing little notes about me on his clipboard. That night I went home hoping against hope that maybe—just maybe—I had a chance.

"You made it!" José shouted across the campus the next day as I met him coming from the gym. "The names are posted on the coaches' door, Tony," he said. "You're on the team!"

My big brother punched me and then hugged me for joy. He wasn't the only Melendez who would play for Chino High. In fact, for the next two years I proudly wore Chino's light-blue jersey and white soccer shorts. Pelé, the great Brazilian soccer star, had no competition from me. I wasn't a great soccer player, but I was okay. As right halfback or fullback, after endless hours of practicing up and down that green, rutted field, I got so that I could use my body, my legs, and my head to lob a ball pretty decently to the waiting forwards.

"Go for it, Tony!" Paolo would yell from the field or the sidelines. "Go for it, Tony!" my brother would chime in from the bleachers, where he sat with Mom, my sisters, and once or twice my dad. "Go for it, Tony!" my little cluster of hope-givers would yell together as I charged up and down the field, trying to be a good team player but hoping secretly that I would eventually make a goal.

One night when we were playing Chino's archrival, one of my teammates kicked the ball straight up into the lights. It was a powerful kick, and I was right under the ball as it fell spinning out of the sky. I looked up, hoping that I could use my head to pass the ball forward, but that ball was falling like a rock. At the last minute I got scared and turned away.

But I turned too late. The ball hit me squarely on the back, knocked me down, and left me gasping. Fortunately, however, the ball careened off me directly into the path of a forward, who kicked it smartly into the goal. I was given credit for a goal assist! Knowing that I had chickened out, I was all the more determined to score a goal on my own.

The next match we played in a southern California cloudburst. After the deluge our field resembled a muddy swamp. Covered in muck from slime-stained soccer shoes to mud-splattered face, I looked like a caveman. This time when the ball landed on the field in front of me, I overkicked and my left leg collapsed from under me. I was out for three weeks while the strained ligaments healed. I had almost given up hope of getting a goal of my own.

Then, toward the end of our season, someone kicked the ball directly at me. It came so fast that I had no time to think. I just kicked hard with my right foot, and the ball shot past the goalie and into the cage.

"You scored!" Paolo yelled. "He did it!" my mother and sisters chimed in. "Good work, Tony!" José shouted from the sidelines.

They say it isn't important whether you win or lose, but how you play the game. That might be true—but what a great feeling it is to score a goal now and then!

MRS. RICHARDS AND THE CHINO CHOIR

Sports and music were at the heart of my high school years. My choir teacher, Mrs. Richards, was in her midfifties. An energetic woman, she accompanied the choir on the piano with her left hand and directed us flamboyantly with her right.

"What are you singing?" she would shout at us, interrupting our four-part harmony in midsentence. "Are you thinking about the words?" she would ask, standing up from the piano bench and marching toward us. "Don't sing until you understand and feel what you're singing about!"

Mrs. Richards believed in me. I had sung in volunteer church choirs in previous years and knew that I had a reasonable voice; but when I tried out for the choir at Chino High, Mrs. Richards got excited.

"You have a wonderful voice and a wide range, Tony," she told me. "Let's develop it. Expand!" she ordered me. "Stretch! Experiment!"

Mrs. Richards had me sing tenor on one piece, baritone on another, and bass on yet a third.

"Understand it?" she would ask me. When I nodded assent, she would add, "Then *feel* it. Quit being lazy!"

Singing for Mrs. Richards was hard work. We performed two major choir concerts each year: one in the spring around Easter time, and one at Christmas. These concerts featured music from the classics and from Broadway shows, but we also did jazz and spirituals, hymns and comic medleys. Every song was choreographed or costumed. We rushed back and forth throughout the concert, changing costumes, makeup, and props.

Without help I couldn't change my costume fast enough during the quick blackouts or brief intermissions, so Dominic assigned himself the job as my dresser. Dominic was a very funny guy who kept the choir laughing with his wild gestures and whispered asides. With olive skin and sandy-brown hair, he looked Hispanic like me, although he was Portuguese. Because we were about the same height and weight, our costumes were interchangeable.

After a scene from *Oklahoma*, for example, we would rush backstage together. Dominic would pull off his cowboy costume and strain into a tuxedo shirt and tails for a medley of *My Fair Lady* songs while I was still struggling to get out of my cowboy jeans. Somehow he managed to dress us both in the half-darkness, fasten both our bowties, lace both pairs of shoes, and pull up both our zippers before we had to race back on stage again.

When the spotlight blazed on after such a transformation, I was always amazed that we were standing there fully clothed (and always a little afraid that in the confusion Dominic had forgotten to get me into something vital—like my pants!).

I loved those choir concert days. We would arrive at the school cafetorium in the afternoon to set up chairs and to lay cables for the lighting. I could use my hips to bump the folding seats into perfect rows, or thread cable around the edges of the room with my feet. We choir members became a kind of performing family and built deep friendships during those rehearsals and performances. When the last song of a concert was sung and the last applause had died away, I was often the last to leave the auditorium, wishing that the songs could go on forever.

MY FIRST ROMANCE

I had informal dates with five or six different girls during my last two years of high school. At first I felt awkward and a bit unsure with the opposite sex. It wasn't easy to walk across the campus hand in hand when I didn't have hands. I couldn't reach out to touch someone without fingers. And there was no way for me to sneak my arm around a girl's waist in the front seat of my car or over her shoulder at a movie or a school play. Yet, I longed to touch and to be touched. I had the same feelings, the same needs, and the same desires that everyone else had.

I tried not to think about it. I looked the other way when my friends and classmates walked by hand in hand. I swallowed my feelings when guys talked about their steady girlfriends. And I stayed away from parking lots or drive-in movies where the kids liked to hold and kiss each other in the semi-darkness. I didn't think that I would ever really fall in love, because I was afraid that no one would ever fall in love with me. I was wrong.

Just six months before my high school graduation, my mother invited Liz, one of my senior-year classmates, to live with us. Her parents were moving to Montana and Liz wanted to finish her senior year in Chino. Liz was friendly, outgoing, and very pretty. Mayella and Marylou adopted her immediately. And though we were in the same high school class and about the same age, I thought Liz saw me as a kind of big brother.

After school one day I found Liz and Marylou sitting together on the front lawn talking. When I walked up to them, Liz suddenly stood and rushed away. I thought I saw tears in her eyes and wondered aloud what might be wrong.

"She likes you, silly," Marylou replied. "Can't you see that?"

I hadn't seen it. How could I see it when I wasn't looking? Besides, she was moving to Montana. I had school, soccer, choir, and a part-time job. Day after day we just passed each other with a pleasant greeting or a smile, until that surprise announcement, "She likes you, silly." For the first time I let myself notice how beautiful Liz was. For the first time I let myself think those thoughts that had been trying to come to life inside me.

"Liz, want to go for a walk with me?" I asked her one afternoon in April.

"Sure, Tony," she answered. "That would be nice."

Her smile and the look in her eyes made me feel weak. I don't know why, but I walked her directly to our church. There was a large, old oak tree in the back of the church. It was a warm, summerlike afternoon, and Liz sat down against the tree trunk and motioned me to sit down beside her.

I don't know what came over me that day, but without an invitation I just lay in the grass at her feet and put my head in her lap. When I finally opened my eyes she was smiling down at me. She reached out one hand and brushed her fingers against my face. For five or ten minutes I just lay there feeling her caress me. It was the first of many intimate times together. I told her all my dreams about the priesthood, about my music, about having a wife and raising a family. During our times together over those last two months of high school, I told her things I had never even allowed myself to think before.

And then the school year ended. In just a few days, Liz would take the Greyhound bus from Chino to her new home in Montana. I felt desperate. I didn't want Liz to go.

"Then let's get married," she said to me one afternoon. "You can find a job in Montana and we could live with my folks. Then when you get settled, we could have a baby and start a family of our own."

I was stunned and excited by her suggestion. To live with Liz forever would be a dream come true.

"But I'm not ready," I answered, my voice weak and unsteady. "I sit around on my rear end playing the guitar. I can't support myself, let alone you and a family."

We stayed up all night talking about the future. I wanted to say *yes!* I wanted to go with her, but down in my heart I knew how easily our wonderful dream could become a nightmare. As the sun began to rise, I knew what I had to do.

"Good-bye, Liz," I said that next day as we drove Liz to the bus depot.

"Good-bye, Tony," she answered. Then she put her arms around me and kissed me. She was smiling but there were tears in her eyes when she turned, climbed up the stairs, and took her seat near the center of the bus. She waved one last time as the Greyhound pulled away. I tried to blink back my tears. I didn't want my family to see me crying, but when the bus turned the last corner and disappeared, I cried like a baby.

Liz is married now. She and her husband and son live in Montana. And though I have loved and been loved several times since that senior-year romance, Liz has a special place in my heart forever.

11. The Spiritual Journey

From the moment I was born, my mother had two choices: she could worry herself frantic about her little boy with no arms, or she could trust God and put my life into his hands. She chose to trust God. Of course, my mother has had her share of worries about me (and I've given her plenty of good reasons to worry), but over the years she has never stopped trusting God to take care of me and to direct my life.

"While you were growing up," she told me recently, "I prayed for you every day."

Mom still prays for me every day. Now I'm old enough to appreciate her prayers, but in my teenage years Mom's spiritual commitment seemed more a curse than a blessing. Let's face it: when you reach that age, you don't care very much about going to church, reading the Bible, or praying with your mother.

I suffered all the normal growing pains that lead to teenage rebellion, but despite my protests, Mom never stopped praying, reading her Bible, or going to church. She even tried to lead her family in times of prayer and Bible study. I remember how she would gather the four of us children around her at the breakfast table or in the living room in an attempt to have some kind of family devotions. At Easter she would lead us from room to room with her Bible in one hand and a devotional booklet in the other, reciting the Stations of the Cross and asking us to kneel and pray as we remembered how Jesus suffered, bled, and died to bring salvation to the world.

She tacked up on our walls calendars with biblical verses or pictures of Jesus and his Family. She planned special meals or celebrations for every holy day that the church celebrates and for every Christian season, from the birth of Christ at Christmas to his resurrection on Easter Sunday. And before going to bed, she would read the Bible to anyone who would sit still long enough to listen. Often we would find her sitting alone in the living room with the Bible in her lap, reading silently and praying for us. I can still remember seeing her, late at night, asleep in her bed with the Bible still open in her hands.

And during my elementary and early junior high years Mom insisted that we go with her to worship. On Sunday mornings she would get us children up, feed us breakfast, and dress us in our Sunday finest. By the time we were out the front door, Dad would be dressed and waiting for us in the car. Even when he was working two full jobs during the week and all day Saturday, Dad would get up early Sunday morning and take us all to church. In Rivas, during their courtship and early marriage, Mom and Dad went to church together, and even when my dad was exhausted or hungover, the Sunday morning family worship tradition continued in America.

THE SUNDAY WORSHIP

Dad, Mom, José, Mayella, Marylou, and I usually sat toward the back of the sanctuary. The other children held a little missal in their hands, while Mom shared her order of worship with me. Mom would kneel to pray upon entering the pew, and then on the padded kneeler before the service began.

Other people ducked their heads for two seconds before sliding to their seats. Mom paused, knelt on one knee, and made the sign of the cross like everybody else; but as she stood, head bowed, at the edge of the pew, you could feel the sincerity and intensity of her prayers. Other people would enter the pew, bounce down on the kneeler, and then bounce right back up again. Mom would enter the row, kneel reverently, and then stay on her knees for silent prayer as the choir took their place in the balcony and the priests and lay readers assembled at the front of the sanctuary.

Sometimes we kids clowned around in the pew before the service began. I could make my sisters laugh without half trying. People sitting near us probably thought that morning worship was a complete waste on me, but I was watching my mother out of the corner of my eye and listening to the worship even then. I was just a child, but I could tell that something important happened to Mom the moment the entrance psalm began.

> "Lord, hear my voice when I call to you.
> You are my help; do not cast me off,
> Do not desert me, my Savior God."

The organ would play and the choir would sing the call to worship. The people would rise as the priest and the altar boys prepared to begin the service. Almost immediately, my mother's eyes would brim with tears—not unhappy tears, but tears of gratitude and praise. I never sensed that worship made her sad or depressed. On the contrary, she was excited by the service. Something wonderful happened in her heart when the people began to sing and pray. And though I was just a protesting child, something wonderful was already beginning to happen to me as well.

The priest's words moved me even then: "The grace of our Lord Jesus Christ and the love of God and the fellowship of the Holy Spirit be with you all." We would echo that priestly greeting with the words, "And also with you."

Then followed the confession of sin: "I confess to almighty God, and to you, my brothers and sisters, that I have sinned through my own fault in my thoughts and in my words, in what I have done, and in what I have failed to do; and I ask you, my brothers and sisters, to pray for me to the Lord our God."

As the choir sang the haunting melodies of the Kyrie Eleison ("Lord, have mercy!"), I always felt a bit confused. I didn't know much about sin then. I was too little to understand why my mother would bow low at the confession, make the sign of the cross, and obviously mean it when she joined in with all the rest, "I have sinned. . . ."

Mothers don't sin, I thought to myself. At least *my* mother never sinned. And if she did lose her temper with us occasionally or tell a gentle lie to protect the man she loved, who would call that sin? Now I understand more. Now I know how it feels to have a loving

God who offers us forgiveness freely for whatever we have done or not done. Now I too bow my head and join in that confession, glad that my loving Father has forgiven me.

"Glory to God in the highest," my mother would sing as the choir and congregation voiced their thanks, "and peace to his people on earth."

Then, following the opening prayers, the reading of the Holy Scripture would begin: "This is the Word of the Lord," the priest would chant. "Praise to you, Lord Jesus Christ," we would join in.

I admit it: sometimes during the reading of the long passages from the Old Testament my mind would wander. Sometimes I would pester my sisters or make them giggle. Other times I would fall asleep in my mother's lap or against the hard, cold pew; but as I grew older, those words of the prophets of Israel calling God's people to follow, demanding justice and mercy for the poor, urging the faithful to remember who they are and why God has called them, got through even to me.

"Happy the people," we sang together at the close of the Old Testament reading, "whom the Lord has chosen to be his own."

Born a Nicaraguan, I had journeyed to America around my first birthday. I was a young Hispanic American with roots in two different worlds being called to live in yet another, invisible world—a world that I could see only in my heart: the Kingdom of God ruled by a loving Father who dreamed great dreams for me.

"A reading from the Holy Gospel according to Saint Matthew," the lay reader exclaimed: "If any person would be my disciple, let him sell all he has, give to the poor, take up his cross, and follow me."

"This is the Gospel of the Lord," the reader would proclaim. "Praise to you, Lord Jesus Christ," we would answer in one voice.

I don't know what was happening to me Sunday after Sunday as the Book was read. I'm sure that my mother must have wondered herself if anything was getting through to her unruly child, but I can tell you now, something was. God's promise is true: the word will not return void. It was being planted in my heart every Sunday of my young life, and one day it would take hold in me and change my life forever.

Every Sunday, after the Gospel reading, the people would remain standing to confess their faith. "We believe in God, the Father almighty, creator of heaven and earth. We believe in Jesus Christ, his only Son, our Lord. . . ."

And every Sunday, even when I was just a little child, I would watch my mother join in that confession. I didn't know what I believed or didn't believe then. It didn't matter. There was belief in my home; my mother proclaimed by her words and by her life that she was a child of God and that we, her children, were God's children too.

I had no way of knowing how difficult those years had been for my mother. I was too young to understand how much she had suffered—or that she was suffering still. She had left her wider family and her friends to emigrate to America to find medical help for me. She had given up her comfortable home in Nicaragua to live in a series of tiny, rundown apartments in the landing path of the Los Angeles International Airport. She had quit her job as an elementary school teacher to raise her family on Dad's minimum wage and the money she could earn from her Amway sales; and when the cash they raised just wouldn't pay the bills, she went to work as a cook in a home for the aged, preparing all three meals for eighty old people for $2.35 an hour.

Perhaps my mother's greatest pain came from watching my father deteriorate right before her eyes. He came to America with his heart filled with dreams: first for me and for the medical attention I could get here, and then for what he might achieve for himself and for his family. Little by little those dreams died. He began to drink even more heavily, trying to escape his growing feelings of helplessness. As he drank more, he became more and more abusive. At first he just yelled at my mother and at us children, threatening us. In the later years those violent outbursts turned into physical abuse.

Looking back, I can see that the only way my mother survived was through her strong belief in a loving, caring God. It was his

Spirit's presence in her life that gave her strength for her painful personal journey.

"Without the Lord, Tony," she said to me one day, "I couldn't have made it."

My mother's Christian faith was and still is at the center of her strength. All these years she has been confident that the Lord knows her, loves her, and has a plan for her life. And she knows that if God has ordained the way she should walk, then God will give her the strength and the courage (whatever she may need) to complete her journey.

"The Lord be with you," the priest would say, beginning an interchange with the congregation.

"And also with you."

"Lift up your hearts."

"We lift them up to the Lord."

"Let us give thanks to the Lord our God."

"It is right to give him thanks and praise."

Those were the words we said together as the priests walked to the altar to prepare the bread and the wine.

"His body, broken for you. Take and eat. His blood, shed for you. Strength for the journey."

I didn't understand Communion then. I still wonder at the mystery of it. What happens when we kneel, full of pain and sorrow, to be fed at his altar? Why, after the simple meal of bread and wine, do we rise up feeling strong again? I can't explain it. Theologians have been arguing about it for centuries. All I know is that when my mother knelt down for Communion, she rose up with new hope in her heart. Somehow the Spirit of God was present in that meal. I could see it in my mother's smile. In that simple act of faith she was strengthened and healed by God's Spirit; and now, years later, when I kneel at the altar and hear those words, "Take and eat," I too feel God's power and experience God's healing in my life.

"Blessed be the name of the Lord," the priest would chant. "Now and forever," we would answer. "Our help is in the name of the Lord," he would conclude. "Who made heaven and earth," we would reply.

Then the organ would strike a great chord.

"The mass is ended," the priest would announce. "Go in peace to love and serve the Lord."

"Thanks be to God," we would reply, and the choir would lead us in the closing hymn.

As a child I loved that closing hymn. It meant that the long time of sitting had ended and that I could get out of the narrow confines of that pew and into the open once again. But even when I complained about going to church on Sundays instead of riding my skateboard or practicing soccer, I knew in my heart that something good happened to me beneath the cross in that old church.

Now I realize that my mother was planting in my heart and in my mind a love for Christ and for his people that has changed my life forever. Thank God that in spite of everything (including my loud and consistent complaints) she never quit trying!

FATHER JERRY DELUNEY

There were parish priests, nuns, and lay workers who also helped show my way to Christian faith. Father Jerry Deluney, a bull-headed go-getter, heads the list of professional Christians who made a positive, lasting difference in my life. Actually, my brother, José, was the first of our family whose life was transformed through Father Jerry's ministry.

José was fifteen or sixteen years old at the time. He was going through a serious state of teenage rebellion. A freshman in high school, José was hanging out with a tough crowd. Already these kids were heavy drinkers. They smoked marijuana and were beginning to explore the more dangerous drugs. Who knows what might have happened to my older brother if Father Jerry hadn't taken a special interest in him?

"She's pretty, isn't she?" Father Jerry said to José one Sunday at the door of the church.

Our parish priest noticed everything and everybody. During sermons he might grab a roving mike, come down from the pulpit, and walk up and down the rows of pews addressing individual members of the congregation by name, asking questions, joking, probing, teaching, leading us to God. José had noticed a beautiful girl in the youth group and Father Jerry took the plunge.

"She's going on retreat this weekend, José," Father Jerry said, grinning. "A lot of great kids will be there. Why don't you join us?"

José was hooked. He rode in the church van to a mountain retreat house, and his life was changed forever.

"I went up there to meet a pretty girl," José remembers, "and instead, I met God."

The family couldn't believe what had happened. José came down from the mountain a different person. He went on several retreats during the next few months and every time he returned, he seemed changed. We didn't know what was happening. José walked around the house on a kind of "spiritual high." Mayella, Marylou, and I were asking ourselves, "What's wrong with this guy? Suddenly, he's nice to us. He talks to us. He hugs us and says, 'I love you' and 'I'm sorry.'"

We didn't understand what had happened to José and I certainly never dreamed that one day soon it would also happen to me. But Mom understood. She watched the changes in José and sneaked away to kneel alone in her bedroom, her eyes filled with tears, and her heart pounding with gratitude for what God was doing in the life of her oldest son.

God used Father Jerry to help answer my mother's prayers about both her sons. "I want you to go on winter retreat with us this year," he said to me one Sunday after mass, "and I want you to give a little speech to the other teenagers who will be there."

I was standing in the parking lot of Saint Margaret Mary's, our church in Chino, looking at our associate parish priest with disbelief in my eyes and a growing sense of doom in the pit of my stomach. I was just a sophomore in high school. I was still in the handicapped classes there, and the retreat was for normal kids. I had never even been on a retreat. And I had never spoken publicly anywhere.

"I can't," I answered, searching for an escape route from this determined priest.

"Sure you can," he countered. "Just drop by my office Thursday after school, and I'll help you." With that, Father Jerry smiled and walked away. Nobody said no to that slender Italian priest with jet-black hair and a machismo mustache.

I worried nonstop for the next four days, but somehow I made it to my priest's little office.

"This is going to be hard for me," I confessed.

"Don't worry about it," he answered. "You'll do fine." And he set about helping me.

I remember riding up into the mountains in a van filled with young people from our church youth group. I remember checking into a cabin and getting a top bunk assigned me in a cabin with a group of eight other boys. I remember games and songs, hikes and Bible studies, campfires, evening vespers, wonderful prayers. But most of all I remember a stone fireplace, forty kids gathered in a semicircle, and Father Jerry introducing me as the evening's speaker.

I froze: I couldn't say anything. I just stood there, staring at them in silence.

"I know this is difficult," Father Jerry said quietly after I had stood there shaking for what seemed like half an hour. "But share with us, Tony, who you are and what you're feeling."

"I'm scared," were the first two words I managed to stammer at my public-speaking debut, "and I'm too numb to feel anything."

Everybody laughed, and a few kids applauded. It was the beginning of perhaps the best talk I would ever give. I followed Father Jerry's cue and just shared what it meant to be me. When I was finished, the kids applauded and then began to ask questions. They wanted to know why I had no arms, how I dressed and brushed my hair, and how I felt about God's allowing me to be born in such a way.

Finally Father Jerry stopped the questions. He stood before us and said quietly, "This was Tony's first talk." Once again the kids cheered and clapped enthusiastically. "He was terrified to stand up here, but he did it," Father Jerry continued, "and because he shared simply and honestly from his own life, each of us has been changed."

The room grew quiet. As the young priest wrapped up our evening together, we all felt that God was there in the room with us.

"That's all God wants from us," Father Jerry said: "to be simple and honest with each other. And when we are, his Spirit enters into our relationships and gives new life."

At the close of the retreat on Sunday, before we loaded into our cars and vans to make the journey back down off the mountain, all the young people crowded around me to hug me and to thank me for my "ministry" in their lives.

That retreat was the very first time I realized that I too could have a ministry. An exciting dream began to take shape inside my heart. Maybe Mom was right: maybe God *did* have a wonderful plan for my life. Maybe God would use what seemed like a tragedy to bring a little good into the world.

BETH ANN

Almost immediately, other people began to appear who would help shape my dream. Beth Ann (now Beth Martinez), our choir director at Saint Margaret Mary's, was one of those important hope-givers who pointed my way toward Christian ministry. Even before I could play the guitar, Beth had me singing with the church choir.

Our church choir was like a second family to me. We met for rehearsals on Thursday nights from seven to nine. By six o'clock I had my skateboard wedged between my shoulder and my chin as I began walking across the dirt roads and vacant lots near our home in the direction of Saint Margaret Mary's. I had to walk and skateboard twenty minutes across the streets and sidewalks of Chino to arrive at choir practice on time.

We gathered in the choir room and drank coffee and punch and talked until Beth said a prayer before the choir rehearsal began.

We would then practice for two hours on an anthem and on our musical responses to the liturgy. Sometimes we sang with the pipe organ; other times we were accompanied by brass fanfares or just a simple, single instrument such as a flute or a guitar.

Our Spanish-style church had stucco walls, a red-tile floor, and a bare wooden ceiling. The music of our little choir echoed through that church and out the open windows. People from the neighborhood would stand outside and listen as we sang. Promptly at nine, Beth would dismiss the rehearsal and we would all adjourn to a nearby McDonald's for food and fellowship. Then I would catch a ride across Chino through the darkness to my home on Essex Street, still humming a liturgical response or rehearsing the words to the next Sunday's anthem.

"You have a wonderful voice, Tony," Beth said to me one evening after rehearsal. "God's going to use that voice of yours, and don't you forget it!"

As I skated home that night, her words played over and over in my mind. "God's going to use that voice of yours. . . ." The idea that God could use even me was beginning to come at me from all directions.

During my sophomore and junior years, I attended four or five weekend retreats. At each retreat I shared my own story and answered questions. And though I was still scared to stand up before a room filled with kids my own age, they all told me afterwards that God had used my words to inspire them. As a result, gradually my nervousness just went away.

Retreat leaders began to ask me to assist them as a small-group counselor. Kids would share their problems with me, and I would answer honestly from my own life experience.

"My dad's a heavy drinker," one boy in a small-group session confessed. "Sometimes he gets violent."

"So is mine," I answered, "and sometimes he gets violent too."

We talked a long time that night about loving parents who are alcoholics, and about learning to live with their disease. That session ended—as they often did—with tears and hugs all around.

"God really used you to help that boy," a young priest told me as we rode down the hill toward home.

I was hearing it more and more: "God is using you, Tony." And little by little I began to believe it.

At the end of each retreat, just before the final mass on Sunday, the young people would gather for our "Going Home" talks. At almost every retreat I would be one of those asked to share something from my own growing Christian faith. One Sunday I talked about the idea that God could use each of us to help bring hope into the world—even somebody with no arms who got scared every time he stood to speak.

After hearing that little talk a friend of mine, Mark Easley, invited me to share a weekend retreat with him at the Divine Word Seminary in Riverside.

THE CALL TO PRIESTHOOD

Los Angeles sprawls across three giant counties, from the Pacific Ocean to the foothills of the San Bernardino Mountains. Near the little town of Rubidoux, on the crest of one of those dry brown hills, is the Divine Word Seminary. Atop the hill stands a giant cross that you can see for miles around. Beneath the cross is a cluster of buildings that includes dormitories, a large dining room and kitchen, a swimming pool for retreats, and a beautiful little chapel connected to a rock-walled parish house where the priests live.

Young men who are considering full-time Christian ministry are invited to attend classes, seminars, and retreats at this preseminary, to experience what life in the priesthood might be. Immediately upon arrival at the Divine Word Seminary I was assigned to the care of a spiritual director, who would be my counselor and friend on that visit and in the months to come. Together we designed a program of prayer, Bible study, Christian service, and witness that would lead to my growth as a Christian and as a lay leader. On each succeeding visit my spiritual director would question me about my progress.

"Have you been able to study the New Testament passages that I assigned you, Tony?" he might ask. "Do you understand them? Is there any one verse or chapter that I might help explain?"

Then he would take out his Bible, his concordance, and his Greek or Hebrew dictionary, and we would work on a passage together. It was great fun. I was a spiritually hungry kid, and he was feeding me spiritual meat that would help me grow.

My spiritual director would also question me about my personal life. "How are you and your father getting along?" he would ask. "How do you handle him when he gets drunk and mean?"

We talked about everything from family relations to sexuality. As my interest in becoming a priest began to grow, we talked about the vows of poverty, obedience, and chastity that I would have to take to enter full-time ministry. To enter Divine Word's college in preparation for seminary I had to promise not to date. But I was a junior in high school. It wasn't easy to talk about celibacy when I was just getting serious about girls.

During our retreats and seminars we would actually experience the life of a full-time priest. We were trained in youth ministries. We would counsel each other; we would teach each other courses on the Bible, Christian ethics, or church history; we would do physical work around the center; and we would help plan and lead the mass.

"We think that you're ready to apply," my spiritual director said one day toward the end of my junior year of high school.

"For the priesthood?" I said, my eyes wide with disbelief.

"For the college," he answered, "and for the four-year preparation that will lead to seminary and eventually to the priesthood."

Although my head was whirling, we talked briefly. I had come so far from that first retreat with Father Jerry, when I stood fearful and silent before the group of my peers. I had passed the test; I had proved myself. God really *could* use Tony Melendez in full-time Christian ministry.

So it was that at the end of my junior-year program at the Divine Word Seminary, my spiritual director sent the traditional letter to Rome, announcing the order's plans for me and passing on my file to their certification committee.

That night, after evening prayer, I walked up the trail behind the seminary and stood alone beneath the giant wooden cross. The sun was setting, and millions of lights were beginning to sparkle across the valley below. I could hear in the distance all those noisy sounds a great city makes, but in my heart there was only one sound: a song of praise. My mom had been right. The promises of Father Jerry, Beth, my spiritual director, and all the others who had encouraged me were coming true. God *could* use a poor Hispanic immigrant with no arms to help bring hope and healing to the world. I would be a priest!

Weeks later my dream came crashing to the ground. I was called into the office of Father Joe Miller. I had expected to hear good news from Rome, but Father Miller didn't smile or look excited. In fact, he looked as if he were about to cry.

"Tony, I have bad news," he said. "Your application for preseminary studies has been turned down. You can enter the college as a candidate for the brotherhood, but you can't become a priest."

I swallowed hard. It wasn't really a surprise; I had kind of expected it, even while I hoped and planned. But I didn't speak. I just sat there in silence, feeling hurt and confused. I wasn't brilliant, but I felt sure that I could learn what needed to be learned. I wasn't eloquent, but already people had been blessed by my little talks and devotionals. I wasn't a powerful or charismatic leader, but I was confident that I could be an able parish priest.

Finally I asked why. Why would the fathers in Rome disqualify me from the priesthood and ruin the dream so many people had dreamed with me? Wasn't there something I could do, some special course I could take, some additional training that would qualify me?

Father Miller hesitated. He picked up the letter, scanned it one last time, then put it down again. When finally he looked at me, his eyes were damp and his hands shook just a little.

"They say you need a thumb and forefinger to serve the Eucharist," Father Miller said. "Without arms, you can't be a priest."

We sat in silence, staring at each other across the letter from Rome.

12. The Life and Death of a Very Good Man

"Chelle, get your *guitarra!*"

How many times I heard those words said to my father when I was just a child.

"*Toca*, Chelle," people would request. "Play for us!"

During a party, reunion, or fiesta, or on a high holy day, family and friends would gather in our living room or in the front yard for food and fun. When the games had ended, when the presents were passed out, when *comida* and *postre* were cleared away, someone would bring out my father's guitar and ask that he sing and play.

"No, no," Dad would answer, shaking his head and waving his admirers away. "Not tonight."

Ignoring his resistance, someone would place the old guitar in my father's arms. The moment his hands closed on that silk-smooth instrument or his fingers brushed across those tight, resonant strings, my dad would come to life. Even as he groaned in protest, Chelle's right hand would pluck the A-string gently while his left hand turned the wooden tuning screw.

The crowd would grow quiet and the children would gather as Dad began to play and sing. He was a natural musician, gifted by God with an ability to play by ear exactly what he heard another guitarist play. In fact, you had only to hum a melody for Dad to play it. He could perform the classics of Segovia or strum and sing the pop tunes of Tin Pan Alley and old Broadway. And the songs of our homeland poured out of him, with their ancient tribal rhythms and their romantic flair.

Our people loved to hear my father sing and play. They were strangers in a strange land. Like our family, they were poor and struggling to survive. They missed the comfort and familiarity of their birthplace. Home seemed so far away, and the future seemed so uncertain; but when my father played and sang for them, a little bit of hope was born again.

Over the years my dad played and sang for us less and less, however. He eventually retired his guitar to a corner of our living room, I suppose because he had less and less to play or sing about. Something began to die in my father the moment he arrived in the United States, and by the time I was a teenager he barely resembled the man my mother had married.

THE GOOD TIMES . . .

When Mom first met Chelle Melendez, he loved life and fearlessly embraced each new adventure. She remembers him as a gentle but passionate man who thought and felt deeply. He had big dreams, and those who knew him best were certain that one day Chelle's dreams would come true.

I still remember those happy moments with my father, when he was his loving, sober self. He was a good and gentle man before his hard life and growing dependence on liquor conquered his spirit and destroyed his dreams. We loved him (and he loved us) very much before the bottle began to rule his life, before the terrible distance began to grow between us.

I remember riding on Dad's shoulders when I still had a cast on my leg after surgery. I remember walking with him around Lake Atitlán, listening to his stories about the mysterious *xocomil.* I remember sitting beside my father as he let me "steer" one of those miniature electric cars that ran on a track at Disneyland; I remember sensing his arm around me and hearing him laugh as I carefully negotiated every turn. I remember feeling excited and proud that this wonderful man was my father.

Before the bottle triumphed, my father loved everybody and everybody loved my father. When he had money, he picked up the tab. Despite his poverty, he laid out the food and drink. He offered his car (when he had one), his house, and his tools to anyone in need. He provided hospitality to strangers, small loans to his friends, and endless support to his growing family. Dad was generous to a fault, and everyone loved him for it.

At Christmas one year my brother begged Dad for a bright-red ten-speed bicycle. The family had no car at the time, and José desperately needed transportation to get to school, to football practice, to his part-time job, and to various distant points around Chino. That special bike was the only gift José had ever really wanted. And though Dad was poor and struggling to make ends meet, when he saw how much José wanted that bicycle, he took on an extra job to earn enough money to buy it.

Dad tried hard to come through for every one of us. For years I had dreamed of driving a car, but by the time I was old enough to be licensed, my father was growing ill. He was too sick to hold down a full-time job, so Mom was working as a cook in a rest-home at less than the minimum wage. There was hardly enough money to pay the bills—and certainly no money for the used car of my dreams.

But the word leaked out. My friends told the world, "Tony needs a car." A stranger who heard about my need called and made an offer. It was one of those mysterious, wonderful moments when dreams that you haven't even dared dream come true.

"I'll loan you $1,500 to buy your car," the woman said over the telephone. "I won't charge you interest, and you can pay the money back as you earn it."

Still stunned by the stranger's generosity, Dad and I bought a used Torino. It was sleek and beautiful, but there was no way that I could drive it without installing a special foot control system that would allow me to steer a wheel on the floor with my left foot while operating the brake and accelerator with my right.

The foot control system would cost $2,000 more. Dad wanted to come through for me, but he didn't have any money—let alone the strength to earn it. As I sat in the passenger seat of the Torino, week after week hoping for another miracle, my father was struggling to find a way. Finally Mom and Dad arranged with a local bank to take out a second mortgage on our home. When Dad showed me the check, we both almost cried. When the foot control system had been installed, my dad and I took a bus to Fresno where the work had been done. At great personal risk, he let me drive the two hundred miles home.

I still remember how proud Dad was, veering back and forth across the freeway with me as I oversteered and then understeered my new Torino. When we reached Chino safely, Dad smiled and nodded in my direction, got out of the car, and disappeared into the back yard for what I suspect was a long drink to calm his nerves.

AND THE BAD TIMES

Even during the last years of our life together, there were wonderful moments when Dad was loving, gentle, and generous. But for the most part, our last years as a family were marred by anger, violent outbursts, and terrible pain.

Up against the physical and mental stress of his new life, my father's body and spirit began to deteriorate. His back injury never really healed. To make matters worse, during one of his late-night stints as a taxi driver he was slashed by a knife-wielding thief; and on his first night of a new job Dad's thumbs were caught and crushed in an industrial magnet that he was cleaning. Because he was alone at the time, Dad had to rip his thumbs free and walk bleeding the five miles home. It's no wonder that he quit playing the guitar: his hands were scarred and callused, and his heart was broken.

My father arrived in this great new land alive with hope. But gradually, as his hope died, Dad began to drink heavily. Somewhere along the way he became an alcoholic. Nobody knows exactly when or where the alcoholism began, but his drinking started innocently enough in Nicaragua, when Dad was still a student. He loved to have a few beers in the evening with the boys. But back then he was a social drinker who could spend a whole night with good friends in conversation, enjoying food and wine, and never show signs of drunkenness.

But after ten years in America, Dad's drinking habits began to change. With his life in disarray, Dad drank not to be sociable but to get drunk, to escape, to anesthetize himself against his pain. When Mom tried to help him quit, Dad hid a bottle in the bathroom or out in the back yard. Actually, we didn't see him drink that much. He tried to hide it from us kids. When we weren't looking, he would steal a drink to fortify himself and to drive away the demons that were pursuing him. And the more he drank, the more angry and abusive he became.

"YOU'RE *NOT* MY FATHER!"

Though Mom spanked us occasionally when we needed it, Dad was always the family disciplinarian. He was educated in Catholic schools where the nuns were very strict. He told us how they struck his extended hands and fingers with a ruler for disobeying school rules. "Spare the rod and spoil the child" became Dad's motto too.

He was "the hand of God" in our life, and "God's hand" struck quickly when punishment was due. When we were small, it was a pinch, a pull of the ear, a sharp, painful tug on a sideburn, a quick slap, or a spanking. As we got older, however, and as his drinking increased, our punishments became more severe. Actually, by anybody's standards—including my father's—we were good kids. We loved our dad, and most of the time we obeyed him quickly. It took just one of his long, hard looks to notify us that we were misbehaving or that we were no longer wanted in the living room; we could take a hint.

But when Dad began to drink heavily, we couldn't move fast enough to suit him. Often after dinner he would slump into a chair in the living room, where we kids might be watching television, doing homework, or listening to the phonograph.

"Go to your room," he would yell suddenly. "All of you!"

"But Dad," José might answer, "it's only seven o'clock. It's early."

With no further warning Dad might surge up out of his chair, hitting José in a fit of rage and again ordering us all to bed. We were stunned, embarrassed, and angered by his occasional violent outbursts. So was Dad—by morning, when he was sober again. Then he would remember the incident and feel guilty.

That's why, on weekends that he didn't work, he kept us on the move. My father knew that he wouldn't drink when he was out with his family. He loved us and didn't want to lash out against us. He knew that if we were together and he was drinking, there would be trouble; so he used those family weekend adventures to hold off the demons that raged inside his head.

On weekends he drove us to the beach, to Disneyland or Knott's Berry Farm, or to the mountains above our home. When there was no money for gas—and not even a spare dollar for the swap meet—we would picnic at a nearby park or beneath the huge bronze tiger mascot at Chaffee School, or we would improvise with neighbors and friends in our own back yard. But on weekends, money or no, we were always on the go. At the head of our family parade my father marched, a kind of Pied Piper—laughing, joking, singing, ordering us about, almost obsessed by his need to keep himself and us on the move.

Eventually, however, he began to carry a bottle even on our family outings. We didn't really see him drinking even on those days together. He tried to hide his bottle, but by evening we could see again that dangerous look in his eyes, and Mom would signal that it was time to head for home.

Being the oldest and the bravest of us children, José became the worst victim of my father's drunken rage.

"Dad, it's too early for us to go to bed," José answered one night when Dad ordered us off to bed so that he could sit alone in the living room and brood.

Dad jumped up and struck José across the face. José stumbled off balance and fell, and Mayella and I just sat there feeling helpless.

"Dad," José said quietly, trying to explain for all of us, "we have homework. We *can't* go to bed yet."

"I said, 'Go to bed!'" my father screamed at him, pulling José to his feet and hitting him once again. "I'm your father. Obey me!"

Hearing that second angry blow, Mom ran into the room to intervene. Mayella began to cry, and I sat on the floor, choking back my own anger. José was crying too, but he stood up bravely. Wiping his tears away, he spoke one last time. "You're drunk," he whispered, "and when you're drunk, you're *not* my father."

For a moment Dad just stood there, dazed. I thought for sure that José would get the beating of his life, but this time Dad didn't move. Sad and confused, he was sober enough to understand what he had done, but too drunk to apologize. Looking back on that moment, I wonder why Dad didn't take José in his arms and say, "I love you, Son. I'm sick. Forgive me. Help me." That we could have handled.

Instead, Dad glared at us. We followed Mom from the living room and left Dad standing there alone. I remember looking back at him in anger. I can still see him in the middle of the room, looking down at his hands and trembling. José was right: that drunken, violent man *wasn't* our father. We could only pray and wait for the day when our real father would return to us.

Our family's life together got worse before it got better. Threats and curses gave way more frequently to angry, violent acts. One early evening in 1979 José and I were entertaining two cousins. We were playing music and sharing stories in the living room. Dad came in from work, heard the noise we were making, and went into the kitchen to fill a large pitcher with water. He was drunk, so we knew what the water was for: occasionally he threw something at the beginning of a violent attack. As he walked through the door, I kicked the raised pitcher from his hand. Dad began to curse and kick out at me so fiercely that José and my cousins had to pin him down and hold him until we could get him calm again.

Another night my father became so enraged that he picked up a heavy electric blender and threw it at me. I was so angry and surprised that I didn't even feel the blow, but that didn't stop me from reacting. To protect myself I used my shoulder to shove him up against the wall. As he struggled to free his arms in order to hit me again, his hand went through the window. Although bleeding profusely, he was struggling against me still.

"Stop it," I yelled. "That's *enough*. You're bleeding."

He fell to the floor, and I managed to wedge him against the wall until he calmed down again.

José continued to be my father's favorite victim as the violent months turned into years. When Dad was drunk, he would tease and taunt, slap and beat my brother without provocation. I often had to throw myself between them to stop the attack.

A DIFFICULT DECISION

On his sixteenth birthday José ran away from home. He found shelter and understanding with the people of our church. Father Jerry, who had witnessed my father's rage, placed José temporarily with an understanding Christian family in our church. Father Jerry tried to counsel my father, but when he wouldn't listen our priest advised my mother to take us children and leave him.

"You and the children are in physical danger," he warned her; and though my mother knew that Father Jerry was right, she refused to abandon the man she loved.

"I couldn't leave your father," Mom told me recently. "He was sick. He would have died without us."

Mom knew that when my father was drunk he was dangerous. She too had been his victim. And though she couldn't leave him, she tried hard to protect us from his violence. She tried never to leave us alone with him; she didn't go out at night so that she could intervene on our behalf if he came home intoxicated and in a rage.

"Those were hard times," she remembers. "My husband's sickness was very bad. I was caught between my children and the man I loved. I knew the dangers, having read and talked to people about alcoholism and abuse. I saw the children's pain, but I couldn't leave him. He had worked hard to support us all those years; he gave up everything he wanted for his own life in hopes of making our lives better. When Chelle drank, it was to escape his pain. He didn't mean to become an alcoholic. He struggled against his illness, but it conquered him; and in his time of weakness I couldn't just walk away."

For awhile it seemed that everything we did made matters worse. For example, as an act of reconciliation, José asked my father to come to his high school graduation. Dad went—but drunk.

"What are you doing here?" José shouted when he saw his father staggering up the walk. "All you ever do is embarrass me!"

Dad left the graduation exercises weeping and ashamed. When I graduated from high school, Dad drove us to the Chino High athletic field, watched us climb out of the car, and then just drove away. He didn't even attempt to share this important event with me or with our family.

DAD'S FINAL DAYS

Alcohol ruined my father long before it killed him. The short highs gave way to longer and longer fits of depression. The poison acted slowly but powerfully to weaken his body and confuse his brain. The more he drank to escape his problems, the worse his problems became. Besides destroying his relationships with friends and family, booze cost my father his position at Parco and kept him too drunk or too ill to hold down even a part-time job to support his family.

Dad stopped drinking two years before he died of cirrhosis, but it was too late. He was weak, jaundiced, and in terrible pain. His belly became hard and distended; his bowels and kidneys began to malfunction. He raged, wept, and hallucinated. It was a long and painful death.

Drinking too much beer, wine, or other liquor can affect every organ of the body. It kills and alters brain cells, blocking memory, dulling senses, and impairing coordination. It can trigger bleeding in the stomach and has been linked to cancer there. It can deteriorate the heart muscle, damage or destroy the immune system, adversely affect hormone levels in both men and women, and lead to birth defects in newborn children.

But of all the organs in the human body, alcohol does the most damage to the liver. Fourteen thousand Americans die each year from cirrhosis, a disease most often caused when alcohol destroys the liver's ability to do its job. The alcoholic's poor liver tries to filter the excess alcohol out of the bloodstream, but because alcohol is high in caloric content, too many calories get by and are stored in the liver as fat. The fat that the liver can't process piles up like garbage in a filter. Clogged and overloaded, the liver cells begin to die. Eventually that vital organ closes down. Cirrhosis leads to a slow, agonizing death. I know: I watched my father die.

Even as he was dying, my father tried to support our family. He walked miles to find help for us from various government agencies. He stood waiting in long lines, hoping to find a program that could bring him relief and his family aid, but there was no help coming. My father had paid his taxes; he was an American citizen whose employers deducted money from each monthly paycheck for twenty years to pay federal, state, and local taxes. The aid that Dad applied for as he was dying was aid that he had earned and that he was qualified to receive. After walking to the welfare office endless times, three to four miles in each direction, my father received a letter approving his request and promising that his first small check was in the mail.

Dad waited almost two years for that check. Even in his last months he continued to make the long walks back and forth to the welfare office, where clerks assured him time and time again that he had been approved and that his check was in the mail. Finally, just days after my father died, his first check arrived. When my mother called to tell the welfare people of Dad's death, they insisted that she return the check immediately.

During the last year of his life my father was in and out of various hospitals and emergency wards. We spent Dad's last Christmas Eve together at San Bernardino County Hospital. Mayella and Marylou decorated a tiny tree, and Mom fixed Dad's favorite Christmas treats. The Air Force granted José a special pass to visit his dying father, so the whole family was together. We gathered around Dad's bedside to sing carols, open presents, and eat cookies.

My father lay there smiling up at us, his eyes filled with tears. The anger and the violence were gone now. We were a family once again, awakening from a terrible nightmare. Mom sat in a chair beside my father's bed. She had loved him through the good times and the bad, and now that he was dying, she was already beginning to feel her terrible loss. Marylou held Dad's hand as he looked around the room. We knew that there was so much he wanted to say to each of us, but he was too ill and too overcome by his own guilt and grief to speak.

We knew what Dad was thinking: he hated what had happened between us as much as we hated it. A good man, he was the victim of forces he couldn't control. And though evil had won a few terrible battles in my father's life, it hadn't won the war.

It was Christmas. We were celebrating the birth of Jesus, who lived and died that we might find forgiveness. Dad didn't need to ask us to forgive him. We had forgiven him already, as we had been forgiven. We stood around his deathbed, knowing that because of our Lord and Savior we would one day be a family once again.

Out in the hospital corridor, carolers were singing:

"How silently, how silently,
The wondrous gift is given.
So God imparts to human hearts
The blessings of his heaven.
No ear may hear his coming,
But in this world of sin,
Where meek souls will receive him,
Still the dear Christ enters in."

Dad was dying; yet my heart was filled with hope. Do you want to know where my hope comes from? I'll tell you. Even on my worst days I'm still hopeful, because of Christmas, Good Friday, and Easter Sunday. In Jesus' life, death, and resurrection, God has forgiven us. No matter how badly I have failed, no matter what wrongs I have done, in Christ I am forgiven. That is the good news (the Gospel). God loves us; God has forgiven us—and that above all else gives me hope!

I visited my dad regularly in the hospital for the next few months, and I prayed for him every day. At the time of diagnosis, the doctors told us that Dad had just a few months to live. He fooled them for more than two long years. Then, at 2:30 P.M. on May 24, 1983, the telephone rang.

"Tony?"

"Yes?" I said, not recognizing the doctor's voice.

"Your father just died. Will you please tell your family?"

I had known for years that Dad was dying, but he had beaten the odds so many times that I thought he would live forever. After all, he was my father. Fathers seem invincible. Suddenly he was gone, and I had to realize that fathers are mortal too. I walked into my mother's room. She looked up and saw the bad news reflected in my eyes.

"He's dead, Mom," I said. "Dad's gone."

She stared at me silently for just a second, then began to weep. "He *can't* be dead," she said, her voice rising from a quiet whisper into a cry that echoed throughout the house. "I wasn't with him."

My sisters and I tried to comfort Mom, but she wouldn't be comforted. She wanted to drive immediately to the hospital to be near Dad. When we arrived at his room on the second floor, he was still lying in the bed as though asleep. We gathered around his body, all of us. After we had mourned in silence for awhile, I kissed him on the forehead and said, "Now you're with the Lord."

SAYING GOODBYE

The parking lot at Saint Margaret Mary's Catholic Church in Chino was packed with cars, vans, and pickup trucks. Inside our family church on Central Avenue the pews were filled with my dad's friends and family. Flowers from those who loved him and who remembered him from better days stretched across the sanctuary. Because I was leading the music, I sat alone to the right of the altar. My mother, my sisters, and my brother sat in the front row. My friend Kent Blair sat in the pew just behind them. Mom was weeping quietly, and Mayella and Marylou were trying to comfort her.

One of the four priests who officiated lifted his arms and spoke the words of welcome: "The grace of our Lord Jesus Christ, the love of God the Father, and the communion of the Holy Spirit be with you all." And the people answered in one voice, "And with your spirit!"

Beautiful prayers were prayed that day, and Mom's favorite Scripture passages were read by friends acting as lay readers. And then, before the short meditation, José, Mayella, Marylou, and I stood to sing. As we sang "Seek Ye First the Kingdom of God," I looked up past the pews and the people, past the balcony where I had sung and played so many times, and past the organ. The sun was still illuminating the beautiful stained-glass window at the rear of the church. Jesus stood outlined against a bright-blue sky bordered in crimson. His robe was crimson too, and on his outstretched hands were crimson marks of the nails that had held him to the cross.

I couldn't see the person in the window to whom Jesus was holding out his bloodstained hands (the balcony railing blocked my view), but as we sang, I felt in my heart that Jesus was holding his hands out to me. I could almost hear him saying, "Tony, without suffering there is no gain. Without death there is no resurrection."

We were all suffering that day. We were feeling the ugliness of my father's death and the long nightmare of his illness. But Jesus was there with us every step of the way, in suffering and in death, giving us hope that one day the pain would end and our family would be reunited once again.

Following the funeral mass, dozens of people drove out to our house on Essex Street. We were really poor at the time. After all, Dad hadn't worked for several years, Mom was still cooking full-time for less than the minimum wage, my governmental assistance check was about $400 a month, and José was away in the Air Force.

But generous women from the church provided food enough for everyone. Even the guests brought drinks, Central American dishes, and desserts. Dad had dozens of faithful friends who sat in the kitchen and living room, in the back yard and in the front yard, telling stories about Chelle Melendez. They were laughing and crying, remembering the good times they had shared with my father.

"Let's get out of here," I whispered to Kent. one of my closest friends since high school.

"Okay," he said, and he didn't even pause or scrunch up his face to make me feel guilty about leaving my own father's wake.

We sneaked out the back door, climbed into my dark-blue 1975 Torino, and drove through Chino's darkened streets. When I'm tired or upset, I like to drive around the countryside or up into the foothills. I didn't feel like talking, so Kent just sat beside me. He knew that if I needed to say something, I would say it.

That night, after my dad's funeral, we drove to a neighborhood bar—the same bar where I played the guitar in my first local talent show two years earlier. We sat at a corner table and talked about my father. I was already beginning to miss him. I had hated him for awhile when he was abusive, violent, and out of his head. But I knew that alcohol had played a terrible trick on my father's brain—that he was really a loving man who had sacrificed a good part of his own dreams that my dreams might come true.

The bar was dark and noisy. I was feeling more and more depressed. So we drove out of Chino and through the foothills up toward Mount Baldy. I drove my Torino off the road at a place where kids park to look out over the city on Friday and Saturday nights. A million lights sparkled all across San Bernardino and Los Angeles counties.

We sat and talked for awhile. Kent's mom had died just a few months back, so he understood what I was feeling. He listened as I poured out my feelings. And when at last the tears came, Kent put his arm around my shoulder and let me cry.

13. Hope to All the People

Looking back over my twenty-seven years, I can remember special moments that changed my life forever. Some of those moments were traumatic and unforgettable; I knew in an instant that life would never be the same. My dad's death was one of those traumatic moments. But there were other turning points that came and went almost unnoticed.

After Dad retired his old Spanish guitar several years before he died, it stood in the corner of our living room like furniture or a piece of art. One evening when I was just fifteen, I leaned down, grasped the old guitar between my neck and shoulder, and carried it into the bedroom that José and I shared.

Looking back now, I realize that when I placed the guitar on the floor at my feet for the first time that night in 1977 and began to brush my callused toes against its strings, one life ended for me and another life began. I saved that moment to talk about until this last chapter because composing and performing music is more a part of my future than it is of my past. Just as my father's song began to die in him, my heavenly Father's song began to come to life in me. And the song of hope that God mysteriously planted in my heart still amazes and delights this singer.

I was a sophomore at Chino High School when I first picked up Dad's guitar, and I was singing in Beth Ann's choir at Saint Margaret Mary's. A guitarist who accompanied the church choir one Sunday morning noticed my interest. I explained to him that on the several times I had tried to strum my father's guitar with my toes, the only noises I made were harsh, unmelodious, and unpleasant.

"You need to tune your dad's guitar to an open chord," he told me, strumming the strings and turning the little tuning screws.

"Now strum this," he said, placing his guitar on the floor in front of me.

When I brushed my big toe lightly across his strings, a beautiful major chord sent shivers up and down my spine. With one quick movement of my foot over six little strings, I had made music that still echoed on the air.

"And you can change the chord simply," he added. "As you place your other foot up or down the fret, a new chord will form."

I placed my right foot on the neck of his guitar, held down the strings, and strummed again. This time the chord sounded higher on the scale than the first. Quickly I moved my foot and strummed again, and a third chord sang from the instrument. I was making music! God used those little chords to open up a whole new world for me.

Later that night, alone in our bedroom, I struggled to tune my father's guitar to that amazing G-chord without my new friend's help. It wasn't easy holding the guitar in place and turning the little tuning screws with the toes on my left foot while simultaneously picking the strings with my right. At first all that my grunting and groaning produced was discord. Then suddenly the strings stretched perfectly into place, and a beautiful G-chord sounded once again.

Today, Dad's old Spanish guitar is my most prized possession. I can't imagine what my life would be like without it. During my last three high school years I practiced on that tough little instrument for four or five hours a day. You can still see the imprint of my heel where it rested on the rounded wooden frame.

Between the two largest toes on my right foot I learned to hold a pick shaped like a triangle with rounded edges. I then formed the chord by pressing the strings down with the toes on my left foot and by strumming with my right. It wasn't easy to learn to play with no hands or fingers, but in a very short time the noises echoing from that old guitar sounded a lot like music.

I admit that my family suffered in the process. I played and replayed each chord a million times—or so it must have seemed to them. From the moment I returned from school until nine or ten at night I practiced, while my sisters watched television or did their homework and my mother worked in the kitchen. Our house is small, and the walls are thin. But my family seldom complained, even though the first few years I sounded pretty terrible.

Beth Ann encouraged me to practice the guitar. As my skills increased, she asked me to accompany the choir or choruses that the congregation sang. Eventually Beth Ann and I even played together for funerals or weddings in our little church. One day she decided that I was ready to accompany a service alone.

I played and sang at a funeral for a sixteen-year-old girl who had died of a heart attack. It was terribly hard to sing without crying. I arrived early and walked by the girl's casket. I knew her: she was part of our youth fellowship, and we had been on retreat together. It was my first closeup look at death, and I rebelled against it.

"What are you doing, God?" I asked as I sat in the choir room waiting for the service to begin. "She was so young. How could you take her?"

During my young adulthood there were bad times—like the funeral of that beautiful young girl—when I doubted God's wisdom and questioned God's will. But there were also times when God seemed so present in my life, and so loving, that I longed to have arms so that I could lift them up in praise. The more time I spent praying and meditating, the happier I became. The more time I spent thanking God for life with all its mysteries, the closer I felt to God. Still, there were those awful times when I sat down in the middle of an empty room and cried, begging God to help me understand the tragedies that were happening all around me.

I remember singing at a second funeral, this time for a teenage boy in Riverside. He was a rock-and-roll singer with his own band. I couldn't wrap my mind around the idea that his song had been silenced before his nineteenth birthday. Once again I cried out to God to help me understand. But God was silent.

After the service the boy's parents invited me to their home. The young man's mother took me into her son's private studio, which was jammed to the ceiling with expensive electronic gear.

"Tony," she said, "I didn't know what to do with my son's music equipment until I heard you sing today. I didn't want someone to have it who might misuse it. Will you take it, Tony? Will you use it in the Lord's work?"

The boy had been killed in an automobile accident. I didn't want to benefit in any way from such a tragedy. Even as I sang at his funeral, I had felt angry at God for letting this happen. There were so many things I couldn't understand.

Then God began to speak to me through the words of the song that I was singing: "Worry not of trouble all around you. Tomorrow will take care of itself. For now, just trust in me."

How glad I was for the words of Jesus in my simple song. During the years that followed, as I watched my own father fall victim to his despair, I spent a lot of time remembering them. "Why, Lord?" I prayed over and over again. "Why can't you heal my father?"

And though my dad never regained his physical health, there were wonderful times of emotional healing. When I was still a junior in high school, Father Michael Manning, a priest with a very successful ministry in media, asked me to appear on a television program being broadcast live from the Anaheim Convention Center. I had played and sung a few times in my own church, but the idea of sitting down before a live audience of 6,000 people and performing on live television at the same time was terrifying.

"Don't worry about it," Dad said when I told him. "We'll go together."

I looked at my father across our little living room. He was smiling at me, and for just a moment I saw the old sparkle appear in his eyes. He was proud of me; there was no doubt about it. My father was happy that I had taught myself to play his guitar. He was excited that in just a few days I would be playing it in a huge auditorium to thousands of people.

Before that moment I hadn't even been sure that he wanted me to play his guitar. He hadn't volunteered to teach me. He had answered a question now and then about music, but when he came home from work he was too tired or too drunk to care. And though I never really hurt his guitar, my heel had to rest on its gold-colored body, and occasionally Dad would ask me to clean and polish it.

My father, Marylou, and I drove through a cloudburst en route to the Anaheim Convention Center that November day in 1979. Traffic crawled slowly across the city. Rain beat against the roof and flowed in torrents down across the windows as the windshield wipers struggled back and forth against the current.

Just off the Santa Ana Freeway at Katella Avenue, our right-front tire went flat. Dad swerved to the edge of the wide, busy road, climbed out into the rainstorm, unloaded the trunk, and began to jack up the car. He asked Marylou and me to stay inside where we would be dry. I could hear him struggling against the rusted lug nuts. He wasn't well, and his injured back still bothered him. He was drenched and breathing hard when he finished, but we made it to the convention center just in time. Father Manning rushed me backstage while Marylou and Dad found a place to sit in the back section of that huge auditorium.

"Ladies and gentlemen," the announcer said, "Mr. Tony Melendez."

The people applauded politely as I walked out onto the stage. When they saw that I had no arms, they grew silent or whispered their surprise. As I sang my one song, I knew that out there somewhere in the darkness my dad was watching and listening to his guitar being played by his son who was born with no arms. I knew the price he had paid to bring me to America, and I knew what that loving act was still costing him in broken dreams and terrible disappointments.

Marylou told me that by the time I had finished my song, Dad's eyes had filled with tears; and when the crowd gave me a standing ovation, he was one of the first people on his feet.

"He clapped hard, Tony," Marylou remembered. "He was soaking wet and trembling, and the tears just rolled down his face."

Before he died, my father was reconciled with my brother as well. Although José had suffered the most from Dad's angry outbursts and occasional acts of violence, there never was a doubt that Dad loved him.

José was still in the Air Force when Dad was admitted to the hospital for the last time, and his commanding officer again gave José an emergency leave of absence to return to California. My father was jaundiced, and his stomach was bloated and hard. He was in terrible pain, but when he saw José, his eyes filled with tears and he struggled to speak those words of reconciliation that he had longed to say.

"I'm sorry," he began haltingly, "for all the things I've done. You know that I love you," he added, "don't you?"

José told me afterwards that Dad wasn't just apologizing for getting drunk. "He was apologizing for all the opportunities we missed to be father and son together," José recalled. "He knew that he was dying. He knew that he had lost the chance to be a real father when I was growing up, and that now he would lose the chance to be a grandfather to my children as well. It broke his heart. He held my hand and wept. And though I had already forgiven him, I wept too for those things that could never be."

Strangely enough, during those awful years of my father's alcoholism and the illness that followed, it was his guitar that God used to comfort me. When my father raged, I sneaked away to my bedroom and played his guitar until my toes bled and my ankles ached. When he lay dying in the hospital, I made up songs in my head to capture and tame the feelings that were raging around inside me. And after he died, at first I played and sang to help relieve the sadness. Later on I played and sang to thank the Lord for getting me through it all.

God was using those times of playing and singing in private to prepare me for my public ministry. At first he used friends like Beth Ann to edge me out of my musical closet. My first real performances were at Saint Margaret Mary's, playing with the choir or for the congregational singing. Then my friend Kent Blair pushed me one step farther.

I don't think a person has many really close friends like Kent in an entire lifetime. We met at a retreat in San Diego when I was sixteen, and he invited me to help his new church choir at Our Lady of Lourdes near Chino. They needed a guitarist to accompany their little group of volunteer singers. Kent said that they seemed really happy when he told them that I had volunteered, but there was one little problem: Kent hadn't told them that I was just learning to play the guitar—or that I played it with my feet. You should have seen their looks that first night of rehearsal when I dropped by.

Weeks later Kent quit the choir and left me in charge. What a shock! I really dumped on him for leaving me, but looking back now, I realize that Kent knew what he was doing. Like Beth Ann, he had forced me to quit playing just for myself in the privacy of my bedroom and to begin growing as a composer and a public performer. During the next months my spiritual and musical muscles were stretched and strengthened, thanks to friends like Kent and Beth Ann who took a risk on me and on the gifts that God had given me.

Several times Kent even risked his life on my behalf. Before I had my Torino, for example, he was the first person who, hearing me say, "Let me drive!" answered, "Why not?" There was no hydraulic wheel on the floor of Kent's car. Sometimes I steered with my knees while he stretched his legs to operate the pedals. Other times he lay down just out of sight and steered "to the right!" or "to the left!" as I directed him, while I operated the accelerator and the brake.

People around Chino knew me well. On my first drives through town they screamed and ran in all directions when they saw me coming.

Several years after pushing me to sing and play at his church, Kent pushed me into performing before the general public as well. He worked at a hospital in Fontana, California, not far from our home in Chino. Near the hospital was the old Steel Workers' Union Hall, complete with stage.

"Let's clean up the abandoned place," Kent said, "and give a family concert."

His idea seemed crazy at first, but in just a few days we had rented the abandoned building and printed advertising handbills to pass out at our churches, at shopping malls, and door-to-door in our neighborhoods. The whole Melendez clan would perform in one way or another. José, Mayella, Marylou, and I would sing. Mom took charge of decorations and ticket sales, while aunts stitched up costumes. José helped create production T-shirts. We rented lights, borrowed a sound system, and got aunts, uncles, cousins, nephews, and nieces to handle the popcorn and soda-pop concession, sell tickets, usher, perform in the chorus, and help clean up the mess. My friend Chris Broadfoot ran the sound equipment, and Kent was everywhere, pulling and pushing the performance into shape.

"One day you'll be making records," Kent said, "and tapes and sheet music and concerts and films and television specials and books."

He rattled on, and we all laughed.

"And on that day you'll need a production company name," Kent added. "What's it going to be?"

"Toe Jam Music," Mayella said, laughing. And though everybody joined in the laughter, the name stuck. On the front of the T-shirts José designed for that first family concert in the Steel Workers' Union Hall (now the Performing Arts Center of Fontana) are the words "Tony Melendez in Concert"; and on the back, for the whole world to see, is written, "Another Toe Jam Production." That name still graces our efforts today.

Five hundred people jammed into that little abandoned union hall to hear us sing. It was a coincidence with deep roots in somebody's subconscious that the night of our first public performance was May 24, 1986, the third anniversary of my father's death. When the drums rolled and the curtains opened, we sang our hearts out for him, sensing that our dad was with the Lord, sitting in the front row of heaven and leading the applause.

At one hilarious moment during that first family concert I stood alone at the center of the stage, right in front of the curtains. The house lights dimmed, and a spotlight lit up the place where I was standing. The majestic fanfare from the movie *2001* played over the stereo speakers. What followed was Kent Blair's idea. I'm not responsible for it, and I don't wish to be blamed if you find the whole idea offensive! But before it was over, the whole audience was laughing hysterically and applauding until their hands were sore.

As the fanfare played, I admitted aloud that once in a while I wished I had arms. Then, as the music grew louder, Kent—still hidden behind the curtains—reached around me with one hand and then another so that I looked for all the world as if I were growing fingers, hands, and arms right before the audience's eyes. At the height of the fanfare, to everyone's amazement I had arms hanging at my side like everybody else's. As I began to talk excitedly of this "miracle," Kent worked his arms perfectly with my voice and body. His hilarious gestures were right on cue (or off cue enough to be all the funnier). And just when I began to believe that they really were my arms and hands, the fanfare sounded again. Slowly Kent withdrew his arms and left me standing there, bowing to the applause.

I often begin a concert now by telling the audience, "You are my hands." It's true. Because I have no hands, I need other hands to help me. I can't pick up a plate of food or put my own coat on a hanger without someone's assistance. I couldn't get along without friends like Kent Blair—but neither could you. You may not need a friend to open a door or close a window, but you need friends just as much as I do to get through the tragic and the comic days ahead.

I thank God for Kent. He and I have slept under the stars at Balboa Beach and in the woods near Arrowhead, joking, laughing, and crying until the early-morning sky turned gray overhead. We've spent hundreds of hours talking about our parents and our girlfriends, about our dreams and our disappointments. We even wrote a song together, "Food Junkie," about our passion for hotdogs and cornchips. We once drove across the country and nearly got arrested for camping too near a high-security military base.

And when a brush fire destroyed the wooden cross above our retreat center in the foothills of the San Bernardino Mountains, Kent and I got our friends together, bought two wooden planks and formed a great, heavy cross, tied it with ropes, and dragged it up the hillside. It took every friend we had to get the cross raised into its two-foot hole and cemented into place; but when it stood there once again, high above the city, we were proud of what we had achieved together. When you're driving through southern California on Highway 18 near San Bernardino, look up into the foothills and see the cross we planted there.

I don't think I would have amounted to anything as a person or as a musician without my friends and my family. And I'm deeply thankful for them, every one. God used each of them in different ways to help me get through the long, hard days and lonely nights.

When I graduated from high school, I didn't know what the future held for me. Once again God used my friends to help me see the way. Our family had struggled to get Dad through his illness and his death. José had finished his term in the Air Force and gone to work driving a semi truck. Mayella and Marylou were still in school. Mom was working full-time at the resthome, cooking three meals a day. Dad's long, drawn-out illness had used up all our funds, and we were struggling to pay the bills. To earn money to supplement the allowance I was getting from a federal grant to the handicapped, I was using my guitar to sing for occasional weddings and funerals, but I needed to make more money. It's hard to get a job when you don't have any arms, however. Even the Church didn't want to employ as a priest a man with no thumb and forefinger.

"Don't worry, Tony," Mom would say. "God has something wonderful in mind for you. Trust God, and don't get impatient."

But I was living off my mother's good will. I was a grown man, and yet my mother was still bringing in the only regular paycheck in the household. I refused to mooch off her. One Saturday Kent and I drove down the Pacific Coast Highway into Laguna Beach, a beautiful little art community on my favorite stretch of California coastline. We parked Kent's car and walked through Heisler Park, past the gazebo near the Las Brisas restaurant, with its spectacular views of the surf breaking over the rocks below.

We walked down the path toward the lifeguard stand and onto Forest Avenue. At the intersection of Forest and the Pacific Coast Highway a young Jamaican was playing his trumpet. I noticed as we walked by that the tourists were throwing coins into his open trumpet case.

"I'm going to play my guitar on the streets of Laguna Beach," I told Kent that evening as we drove back toward Chino.

Kent smiled and nodded. "Why not?" he said.

The very next weekend Kent and I drove back to Laguna Beach. We parked on the hillside, where there were no parking meters, and walked down to Forest Avenue. Kent was carrying my guitar case; I was walking beside him, muttering to myself.

"I can't do this," I said. "It makes me feel like a beggar."

"Then don't," Ken said supportively. "There are other ways to make a buck."

"I *have* to do it," I whispered. "I feel like low-life, a scum-bucket, a bum," I added, "but I *have* to do it!"

Kent opened my guitar case and spread a piece of canvas for my guitar. I sat down on a bench on Forest Avenue, swallowed hard, and began to play. At first nobody seemed to notice. Then Kent walked up to me and put his own dollar in the open case. I frowned at him and felt embarrassed, but the people were beginning to gather.

I began to sing the first song that I had ever written. Like so many of my songs, "Hands" is a prayer. It's the story of Jesus' death: the scars, the nails, and the wounds. And tourists and towns-folk stopped to listen.

"My Lord has died for me," I sang quietly, and cars and vans filled with shoppers and sightseers slowed down. Windows were rolled down; a camera clicked.

"God wants to take my hands," I sang, "but I'm so caught up in this world that I just won't take his hand."

When the song ended, there was applause and the clink of money in my guitar case. During one song, when nobody else was looking, I spotted Kent reaching down into the case. He took his own dollar back and grinned at me.

For about four months I sang on that streetcorner in Laguna Beach three or four days a week to help earn money to pay our family's bills. There were exciting moments when people stopped to tell me how much my singing had encouraged them. One man even dropped in a $100 bill. But most of the time I felt embarrassed to be singing there. I wondered if this would be my future: singing for quarters thrown into my open guitar case. My dad had given up everything to bring me to America when I was just a baby so that I wouldn't end up begging on the streets of Nicaragua. Now I felt that I was begging with my music on the streets of Laguna Beach.

"Don't worry, Tony," Mom repeated. "God has something wonderful in mind for you. Trust God, and don't get impatient."

It was at this time that a letter came out of nowhere asking me to audition to sing for Pope John Paul II on his visit to America. For seven years my mom had encouraged me. She never once stopped believing that God was at work in my life and that God's plan was worth waiting for. But I never dreamed during those months of playing and singing on the streetcorner that my very next gig would be before the pope himself, and for tens of millions of people in a television audience that stretched around the globe.

Then suddenly I was there, sitting on that little red platform built especially for me in the middle of the Universal Amphitheater in Hollywood, California. My friend Kent was watching from his house in Chino. My mom and sisters were sitting in the living room of our home on Essex Street. My girlfriend, Nettie, was in the last row of the "nosebleed" section, high in the highest balcony of that 6,000-seat amphitheater.

"Now, Holy Father," a young man's voice echoed across the audience to the place where the pope sat smiling, "we have a special gift that we would like to present to you."

Kent told me later that he began to cry when the spotlight lit up the place where I was sitting.

"Our gift represents courage," the boy's voice continued, "the courage of self-motivation and family support."

My mom and sisters told me afterwards that as the introduction concluded, they were holding each other on the sofa and blinking back their tears.

"The gift is music," the boy added, "in a performer who says when he sings, 'I hear the Lord.'"

At that moment I lifted my feet to the strings of my father's old guitar, and I knew that somewhere in heaven he was crying too—tears of joy for what God had done to answer my mother's prayers for all of us.

"Holy Father," the young man concluded, "we are proud to present to you Tony Melendez."

The crowd applauded and I began to play and sing:

> "The day is filled with love.
> Today is like no other day before,
> And you and I will never be the same.
> I give you all my love this day and every day,
> Forever and forever, in our joys and in our pain."

The orchestra joined in on the second verse, and the audience began to clap in time with the music. When I finished the song, the crowd leaped up, applauding. Even the pope stood, and to everyone's surprise he began to make his way across the barricades to stand at my feet. The next thing I knew he was reaching out to hold me and to kiss me. The audience was weeping and applauding. Back home my mother was holding up her arms in praise, tears streaming down her face too.

Just days before I had been singing on the streets of Laguna Beach and wondering if I would spend my life there singing for quarters. I didn't know it then, but in the days ahead I would be singing in churches and public auditoriums, on television specials broadcast live from coast to coast, and on concert tours across America, in Europe, and in the Orient. There would be a book on my life, and a movie of the week on network television. At that moment, while I sat in the spotlight listening to the cheers of that great crowd, God was changing my life forever.

I could hear Mom's words: "Don't worry, Tony. God has something wonderful in mind for you. Trust God, and don't get impatient."

Then, straining to be heard above the noisy, happy crowd, the pope said to me, "Tony, you are truly a courageous young man. You are giving hope to all of us. My wish to you is to continue giving this hope to all the people!"

Years earlier the letter from the Vatican had refused my request to study for the priesthood because I had no thumb or forefinger with which to hold the bread and the wine. How sad and disappointed I had been. And yet now the Holy Father himself was blessing me for my ministry.

"Hope to all the people!" he had said.

One moment I was feeling that my life had no future, that I would end up practically begging on the streets; and at the next moment I was singing and playing the Good News to crowds of people all around the world. That's the mystery: God is at work in our lives even when we don't feel him there. Now if we could just learn to trust God's promises and depend upon God's Word!

Just a few weeks ago I returned to the Universal Amphitheater to sing again. After the concert I walked backstage through the waiting crowd of old friends and new, past reporters and television camera crews, past guards and curious fans.

At the back of the crowd I saw a badly deformed young woman in a wheelchair. Her arms and legs were twisted, but she smiled and tried to wave as I passed. I kept walking toward the exit; then I stopped, turned around, and walked back in her direction. When she saw me standing beside her, her eyes filled with tears. She reached her hand out toward me and struggled to speak.

"Tony," she said, "because of you, we all have hope!"

I smiled and mumbled something. I didn't know what to say. I wanted to hold her in my absent arms and let my tears mingle with hers. Instead, armless, I thanked her and walked away.

It's a mystery, isn't it, that God could use this armless kid from Nicaragua to bring hope to anyone? Though I don't understand it, I know that it's true. And God can use me, God can also use you. That's the hope we share. God loves each of us, and if we let him, God will use us to bring a little hope, a little love, a little peace into our broken and dying world.

And when you get discouraged, when you fail or are afraid, remember what my mother said to me over and over again: "Don't worry. God has something wonderful in mind for you. Trust God, and don't get impatient!"

Epilogue

In the last nine and a half years since John Paul II reached out to kiss my cheek, my whole life has been turned upside down. Maybe I should say right side up, but in fact, I know God had something in mind for me.

Before that evening at the Universal Amphitheatre when the whole world seemed to hear me sing, I was unknown, life was slow, relaxed and rather comfortable. I enjoyed leading the choir at church, and music somehow took care of my financial needs. Nobody bothered me in the evenings when I sat in my house on Essex Street writing songs and practicing my guitar.

Now all of that has changed. From that moment when John Paul II applauded my song and commissioned me to bring hope to all the people, our phone has not stopped ringing. Overwhelmed with calls, I asked my brother José to assist in this new and exciting endeavor. He quit his job and became my business partner. We established our company and ministry, calling it Toe Jam Music. José helped to organize and manage all the work—it never seemed to stop, and he began to travel with me full-time.

Since then I have travelled to fourteen foreign countries and forty-nine states in the United States, making countless television appearances, including *The Today Show, Good Morning America, Geraldo, CBS This Morning, The Late Show with Arsenio Hall, 700 Club, Robert Schuller's Hour of Power,* and prime-time network specials for Variety Clubs and Very Special Arts. I also performed at the World Series, where I sang the National Anthem for the fifth game of the 1989 series. I've made numerous major personal appearances; and newspaper and magazine articles have appeared on me throughout the world.

Eventually, I had the opportunity to share three additional performances for papal gatherings. The first occurred on a trip to Rome when I was able to attend an audience with the Pope at the Vatican. At the end of the audience, the Pope remembered me and embraced my head saying, "Oh, my friend from Los Angeles." Next, I performed in the Pope's homeland of Poland for World Youth Day in 1991, a gathering of almost two million people, and again for World Youth Day 1993 in Denver, Colorado, before the Vigil and after the Mass.

It has been my privilege to be invited to share my music and message for numerous church-related functions and spiritual gatherings, having the ability to cross the bridge over religious barriers. I have also received numerous awards and honors, including special commendations from President Reagan, the State of California, the City of Los Angeles, Variety Clubs of America, Very Special Arts, and countless other civic and charitable organizations. I also received the first annual Inspirational Hero Award from the NFL Alumni Association at Super Bowl XXIII in Miami.

In 1989, I recorded my first album, a collection of contemporary Christian songs entitled *Never Be the Same,* which resulted in nominations for Best New Artist of the Year from *Cashbox Magazine* and the Gospel Music Association. My Spanish LP, *El Muro Se Cayo* (The Walls Came Tumblin' Down), was released by Latin radio stations across the country. *Ways of the Wise,* my second Christian album, includes the musical talents of Gary Chapman and Phil Keaggy. The fall of 1990 *CCM* (Contemporary Christian Music) *Magazine's* Top Pop List charted *Ways of the Wise,* my first single released from the album, at #3. By December of 1996, my third and most current Christian album will have been released, entitled *Take My Hand.*

As a performer who is managing to find a niche in several different media, my voice was featured in an animated video, *Why Christmas Trees Aren't Perfect,* released in the fall of 1990. The project includes a duet between Jodi Benson (the voice of Ariel in *The Little Mermaid*) and myself. And with the publication of my autobiography, *A Gift of Hope,* by Harper & Row in 1989, I became, by the grace of God, and with the help of my editors, a bestselling author.

My new-found singing career also brought changes in my personal life. During a concert tour through Dallas, Texas, I was introduced to Lynn Zechman who shared my love for God and music. I married that beautiful young lady in the summer of 1990, and we have vowed to love and honor each other, for the rest of our lives. Lynn and I now reside in the Dallas area, along with our greatest blessing, our daughter Marisa. We are often in awe of the graces God has bestowed on us.

I won't lie to you—my faith has been challenged. It is very easy to get caught up in the fame and the glory, with everybody catering to your every need. I have learned how important it is to surround myself with loved ones. They keep me on the right path of humility, and I have realized that all the prayers of my friends and family have strengthened me beyond words.

There have been times during a concert that I have felt so caught up in the lyrics and the emotion of the song, that the tears just pour down off my face. I can remember sharing personal moments of my family and struggling to keep my composure. The crowd just simply sits and listens, taking it all in, as if they themselves have gone through a similar situation. Sometimes I can see their faces as they wipe tears off their cheeks. By the end of the evening some people feel compelled to embrace me, then walk away, unable to say anything but "thank you."

God is in total control. I am His instrument and He is the musician. Without His gentle hands strumming my life, there would be no harmony in this delicate instrument. So tell me, how is it that a person with no hands has been able to inspire in ways that can change the whole outlook of a person's life? I have no words of wisdom or healing powers, but God shines through my songs, and I feel His presence every time I sing.

Amidst the "celebrity status," I'm hoping people can see a simple-hearted singer trying to do his best to serve God. What I want most out of life now is to be a good husband and father, and to be able to continue to allow God to use me as His instrument. I don't know exactly how God does it, but when the lights go down and I walk out on that stage to sing and play, hope begins to grow like a tiny seed in the hearts and minds of those who watch. It is something mysterious that God does, and every time it happens, I thank God for the gift of hope that He has planted in each and every one of our lives.